MEDIÆVAL LATIN LYRICS

MEDIÆVAL
LATIN LYRICS

by

HELEN WADDELL

W · W · NORTON & COMPANY · INC ·
NEW YORK

Library of Congress Cataloging in Publication Data

Waddell, Helen, 1889-1965, comp. and tr.
    Mediaeval Latin lyrics.

    Latin and English.
    Includes bibliographical references.
    1.   Latin poetry, Medieval and modern.   2.   Latin
poetry, Medieval and modern—Translations into English.
3.   English poetry—Translations from Latin.   I.   Title.
PA8164.W3   1977   874'.03'08   77-8629
ISBN 0-393-04493-9

ISBN 0-393-00873-8 (pbk)

PRINTED IN THE UNITED STATES OF AMERICA

2   3   4   5   6   7   8   9   0

PREFACE

THE introduction to this collection of mediæval Latin verse
was written some years ago in *The Wandering Scholars*, which
proved in the end to be not so much a study of the
Vagantes as a long digression, a kind of imperfect history of
mediæval lyric. The excuse for that long digression is in
the half-articulate melody of the fragments of earlier verse
that follow, as timid in comparison with the ease of twelfth
and thirteenth century lyric as Sir Thomas Wyatt's un-
certain plucking at the strings with the flawless resonance
of Campion. Yet the one is the begetter of the other.
The lyric of the great age, 1150 to 1250, has secret springs,
and scholars have made a good, if non-proven, case for
Celtic and Arabic; but the deepest source is in the pagan
learning that flows like a sunk river through the mediæval
centuries, the " ancient fields " whither Alcuin rose from
his bed to go morning after morning, thumbing the sleep
from his eyes (*discutit ex oculis nocturnos pollice somnos*), with
the dawnlight fresh on the sea—

> *Splendida dum rutilat roseis Aurora quadrigis*
> *Perfundens pelagus nova luce liquidum.*

It is for the sake of the unbroken tradition that the
Virgilian *Copa* and a handful of lyrics of the Silver Age
have been included, verse that by no straining of chronology
could be called mediæval. They are here because by means
of them the line of descent can be more clearly traced;
they were the wayfaring-tree, the *lenta viburna* that could
bear transplanting, where the cypress of the greater Roman
verse must stand solitary. Petronius is closer to the first
Italian sonnet writers than he is to Horace; and in the
anthologies of the Codex Salmasianus and the lost Beauvais
manuscript of Isidore, as well as in Ausonius, the secret
romantic quality of Latin, "*praeclusi viam floris*," is unsealed.
The mediæval Venus is less the royal goddess of the *Aeneid*

than the glimmering gracious figure of the *Pervigilium Veneris*, the Dione of the April woods: in lyric after lyric the lovers cry to her by the lovelier name—

" *Et quibus es Venus*
Esto Dione."

Yet in anthologies omission is a worse thing than inclusion: and the omissions here may well seem unaccountable. There are five lyrics from Fortunatus, but not the two that are his immortality: Hrabanus Maurus is here, but not his pupil and far greater poet, the ill-starred Gottschalk: there is no trace of the glorious rhythms of " *O Roma nobilis orbis et domina,*" nor of Hildebert who has the antique gravity, nor of Gautier de Châtillon, and only a single lyric from the tiny but precious collection of the Arundel MS. I tried to translate them, and could not. To those born with this kind of restlessness, this curiosity to transmute the beauty of one language into another, although this baser alchemy is apt to turn the gold to copper and at worst to lead, a great phrase in the Latin, something familiar in the landscape, some touch of almost contemporary desire or pain, may waken the recreative trouble; yet a greater phrase, a cry still more poignant, may leave the mind the quieter for its passing. A man cannot say " I will translate," any more than he can say " I will compose poetry." In this minor art also, the wind blows where it lists.

In one thing the translator is happy: he walks with good companions. He is a kind of Old Mortality, his business, like Radulfus Glaber when they harboured him at St. Germain d'Auxerre, to go about with hammer and chisel, reviving the defaced inscriptions on the tombs of his brethren. Places where men have once been and now are not are older and more sacred, but at the same time friendlier, than virgin soil that has no history. And these poems, preserved by the piety of old monastic houses now themselves decayed, and printed in the last hundred years by scholars as patient as the men who first transcribed them, Thomas Wright and Edelstand du Méril and Ernest Dümmler, Ludwig Traube and Wilhelm Meyer and Paul

vi

von Winterfeld (to make mention only of the dead), are after all but epitaphs of their first makers: and like all mediæval epitaphs, they cry out for that remembrance that is itself a prayer. There is no longer either tomb or inscription in what was once the Abbey of St. Martin at Tours; but in his *Lament for the Cuckoo*, his *Winter* and his *Epitaph*, still " *lieth the Lord Abbot Alcuin of blessed memory, who died in peace on the nineteenth of May.*"

To the unwearied patience of Mr. Saintsbury and Mr. Gregory Smith, who read the proofs of the earlier book and have continued that good office for the second, and of Miss H. L. Lorimer and Mr. C. J. Fordyce, I owe an unusually heavy debt. Whatever assault these versions still commit upon the older language, it is not for lack of warning and good counsel, and such blunders as still remain, because the mould of the verse had set and I was too obstinate to break it, seem small to me in respect of those from which their knowledge delivered me.

The biographical notes appended cover something of the same ground as *The Wandering Scholars*, but with more detail. The account of the estrangement between Ausonius and Paulinus of Nola is taken from the earlier book, and a few lyrics which have already appeared in it are included here for the sake of completeness. For books on the subject other than the original sources given in the notes, the reader is referred to the list at the end of the *Scholars*, and, especially for the more sober poets, to the remarkable bibliography in Mr. F. J. E. Raby's *History of Christian Latin Poetry* (Oxford, 1927). Valuable books which have been published since then are Mr. Stephen Gaselee's *Oxford Book of Medieval Latin Verse* (1928); Professor P. S. Allen's *The Romanesque Lyric* (University of North Carolina Press, 1928); the Abbé Tardi's *Fortunat* (Paris, 1927); and *Vagantenlieder*, Ulich and Manitius (Jena, 1927), which supplies a very much needed text for some poems at least of the *Carmina Burana*, of which Schmeller's edition, first published in 1847, has earned the obloquy and affection of eighty years.

HELEN WADDELL.

PRIMROSE HILL, *August*, 1929.

POSTSCRIPT

In the years since 1929 I have had suggestions and help in revision from many readers, notably Mr. C. J. Fordyce and Mr. J. H. Mozley; and from Henry Broadbent and Sir Frederick Pollock, *bonae memoriae*. Only two sections of the definitive text of the *Carmina Burana* (Hilka and Schumann, Heidelberg, 1930) have as yet been published: but I have gratefully taken advantage of it in such poems as were available. Some account of material published since 1927 will be found in the revised bibliography to the sixth edition of *The Wandering Scholars*.

The intervening years have made more apparent to me the justice of a complaint brought by a discriminating critic against the principle of selection in this anthology: that it has preferred " the hilarity and mockery of the last masks of paganism "—a harsh phrase for verse as innocent as Herrick's—to the *sanctum saeculare* of the mediæval hymns. Yet it is a preference in seeming only. The greatest things in mediæval Latin, its " living and victorious splendours," are not here, because I cannot translate them. Even in secular Latin there are things before which translation is abashed: for these others, *nondum propalatam esse viam sanctorum*: " the way into the holiest of all was not yet made manifest."

H. W.

April, 1948.

MEDIÆVAL LATIN LYRICS

APPENDIX VERGILIANA

Copa Surisca

Copa Surisca caput Graeca redimita mitella,
  crispum sub crotalo docta movere latus,
ebria fumosa saltat lasciva taberna
  ad cubitum raucos excutiens calamos.
quid iuvat aestivo defessum pulvere abesse,
  quam potius bibulo decubuisse toro?
sunt scaphia et kelebes, cyathi, rosa, tibia, chordae,
  et triclia umbrosis frigida harundinibus.
en et, Maenalio quae garrit dulce sub antro,
  rustica pastoris fistula more sonat.
est et vappa cado nuper defusa picato
  et strepitans rauco murmure rivus aquae.
sunt etiam croceo violae de flore corollae,
  sertaque purpurea lutea mixta rosa,
et quae virgineo libata Achelois ab amne
  lilia vimineis attulit in calathis.
sunt et caseoli quos iuncea fiscina siccat,
  sunt autumnali cerea pruna die.
castaneaeque nuces et suave rubentia mala,
  est hic munda Ceres, est Amor, est Bromius.
sunt et mora cruenta et lentis uva racemis,
  et pendet iunco caeruleus cucumis.
est tuguri custos armatus falce saligna,
  sed non et vasto est inguine terribilis.

APPENDIX VERGILIANA

Dancing Girl of Syria

DANCING girl of Syria, her hair caught up with a fillet:
Very subtle in swaying those quivering flanks of hers
In time to the castanet's rattle: half-drunk in the smoky
    tavern,
She dances, lascivious, wanton, clashing the rhythm.
And what's the use, if you're tired, of being out in the dust
    and the heat,
When you might as well lie still and get drunk on your
    settle?
Here's tankards and cups and measures and roses and pipes
    and fiddles
And a trellis-arbour cool with its shade of reeds,
And somewhere somebody piping as if it were Pan's own
    grotto,
On a shepherd's flute, the way they do in the fields.
And here's a thin little wine, just poured from a cask that
    is pitchy,
And a brook running by with the noise and gurgle of
    running water.

There's even garlands for you, violet wreaths and saffron,
And golden melilot twining with crimson roses,
And lilies plucked where they grow by the virgin river,
—Achelois brings them in green willow baskets—
And little cheeses for you that they dry in baskets of rushes,
And plums that ripen in the autumn weather,
And chestnuts, and the cheerful red of apples.
In brief, here's Ceres, Love, and rowdy Bacchus
—And red-stained blackberries, and grapes in bunches,
And hanging from his withe seagreen cucumber.
And here's the little god who keeps the arbour,
Fierce with his sickle and enormous belly.

3

huc Calybita veni, lassus iam sudat asellus,
  parce illi, Vestae delicium est asinus.
nunc cantu crebro rumpunt arbusta cicadae.
  nunc vepris in gelida sede lacerta latet.
si sapis, aestivo recubans te prolue vitro,
  seu vis crystalli ferre novos calices.
heia age pampinea fessus requiesce sub umbra
  et gravidum roseo necte caput strophio;
per morsum tenerae decerpens ora puellae.
  a pereat cui sunt prisca supercilia!
quid cineri ingrato servas bene olentia serta?
  anne coronato vis lapide ista tegi?
pone merum et talos. pereat qui crastina curat.
  Mors aurem vellens, " vivite," ait, " venio."

Hither, O pilgrim! See, the little donkey
Is tired and wistful. Spare the little donkey!
Did not a goddess love a little donkey?

It's very hot.
Cicadae out in the trees are shrilling, ear-splitting,
The very lizard is hiding for coolness under his hedge.
If you have sense you'll lie still and drench yourself from
    your wine cup,
Or maybe you prefer the look of your wine in crystal?
Heigh ho, but it's good to lie here under the vines,
And bind on your heavy head a garland of roses,
And reap the scarlet lips of a pretty girl.
—You be damned, you there with your Puritan eye-brows!
What thanks will cold ashes give for the sweetness of
    garlands?
Or is it your mind to hang a rose wreath upon your
    tombstone?
Set down the wine and the dice, and perish who thinks of
    to-morrow!
—Here's Death twitching my ear, " Live," says he, " for
    I'm coming."

PETRONIUS ARBITER

Parvula securo tegitur mihi culmine sedes
uvaque plena mero fecunda pendet ab ulmo.
dant rami cerasos, dant mala rubentia silvae,
Palladiumque nemus pingui se vertice frangit.
iam qua diductos potat levis area fontes,
Corycium mihi surgit olus malvaeque supinae
et non sollicitos missura papavera somnos.
praeterea sive alitibus contexere fraudem
seu magis imbelles libuit circumdare cervos
aut tereti lino pavidum subducere piscem,
hos tantum novere dolos mea sordida rura.
i nunc et vitae fugientis tempora vende
divitibus cenis. me si manet exitus idem,
hic precor inveniat consumptaque tempora poscat.

PETRONIUS ARBITER

SMALL house and quiet roof tree, shadowing elm,
Grapes on the vine and cherries ripening,
Red apples in the orchard, Pallas' tree
Breaking with olives, and well-watered earth,
And fields of kale and heavy creeping mallows
And poppies that will surely bring me sleep.
And if I go a-snaring for the birds
Or timid deer, or angling the shy trout,
'Tis all the guile that my poor fields will know.
Go now, yea, go, and sell your life, swift life,
For golden feasts. If the end waits me too,
I pray it find me here, and here shall ask
The reckoning from me of the vanished hours.

7

PETRONIUS ARBITER

O LITUS vita mihi dulcius, o mare! felix
  cui licet ad terras ire subinde meas!
o formosa dies! hoc quondam rure solebam
  Naiadas alterna sollicitare manu!
hic fontis lacus est, illic sinus egerit algas:
  haec statio est tacitis fida cupidinibus.
pervixi: neque enim fortuna malignior unquam
  eripiet nobis quod prior hora dedit.

PETRONIUS ARBITER

O SHORE more dear to me than life! O sea!
Most happy I that unto my own lands
Have leave to come at last.   So fair a day!
Here it was long ago I used to swim
Startling the Naiads with alternate stroke.
Here is the pool, and here the seaweed sways.
Here is the harbour for a stilled desire.
Yea, I have lived: never shall Fate unkind
Take what was given in that earlier hour.

PETRONIUS ARBITER

LECTO compositus vix prima silentia noctis
   carpebam et somno lumina victa dabam,
cum me saevus Amor prensat sursumque capillis
   excitat et lacerum pervigilare iubet.
" Tu famulus meus," inquit, " ames cum mille puellas,
   solus, io, solus, dure, iacere potes? "
exsilio et pedibus nudis tunicaque soluta
   omne iter ingredior, nullum iter expedio.
nunc propero, nunc ire piget, rursumque redire
   poenitet, et pudor est stare via media.
ecce tacent voces hominum strepitusque viarum,
   et volucrum cantus fidaque turba canum:
solus ego ex cunctis paveo somnumque torumque,
   et sequor imperium, magne Cupido, tuum.

PETRONIUS ARBITER

Laid on my bed in silence of the night,
  I scarce had given my weary eyes to sleep,
When Love the cruel caught me by the hair,
  And roused me, bidding me his vigil keep.
" O thou my slave, thou of a thousand loves,
  Canst thou, O hard of heart, lie here alone? "
Bare-foot, ungirt, I raise me up and go,
  I seek all roads, and find my road in none.
I hasten on, I stand still in the way,
Ashamed to turn back, and ashamed to stay.
There is no sound of voices, hushed the streets,
  Not a bird twitters, even the dogs are still.
I, I alone of all men dare not sleep,
  But follow, Lord of Love, thy imperious will.

PETRONIUS ARBITER

Sɪᴛ nox illa diu nobis dilecta, Nealce,
    quae te prima meo pectore composuit;
sit torus et lecti genius secretaque lampas,
    quis tenera in nostrum veneris arbitrium.
ergo age duremus, quamvis adoleverit aetas,
    utamurque annis quos mora parva teret.
fas et iura sinunt veteres extendere amores;
    fac cito quod coeptum est, non cito desinere.

PETRONIUS ARBITER

NEALCE, be that night for ever dear,
   The night that laid you first upon my heart.
Dear be the couch, the quiet burning lamp,
   And you, so tender, come into my power.
Still let us love, although the years be hasting,
And use the hours that brief delay is wasting.
Old love should last: O Love, do thou forfend
That what was swift begun, were swift to end.

PETRONIUS ARBITER

Foeda est in coitu et brevis voluptas,
et taedet Veneris statim peractae.
non ergo ut pecudes libidinosae
caeci protinus irruamus illuc
(nam languescit amor peritque flamma);—
sed sic sic sine fine feriati
et tecum iaceamus osculantes.
hic nullus labor est ruborque nullus:
hoc iuvit, iuvat et diu iuvabit;
hoc non deficit incipitque semper.

PETRONIUS ARBITER

DELIGHT of lust is gross and brief
  And weariness treads on desire.
Not beasts are we, to rush on it,
  Love sickens there, and dies the fire.
But in eternal holiday,
Thus, thus, lie still and kiss the hours away.
No weariness is here, no shamefastness,
Here is, was, shall be, all delightsomeness.
And here no end shall be,
But a beginning everlastingly.

PETRONIUS ARBITER

Si Phoebi soror es, mando tibi, Delia, causam,
  scilicet ut fratri quae peto verba feras:
" marmore Sicanio struxi tibi, Delphice, templum,
  et levibus calamis candida verba dedi.
nunc si nos audis atque es divinus, Apollo,
  dic mihi, qui nummos non habet, unde petat."

PETRONIUS ARBITER

SISTER art to Phœbus, Lady Moon?
   Then, I pray you, take to him my prayer.
" God of Delphi, of Sicilian marble
   I have built a fane to worship there,
I have sung a shining song and piped it
   On a slender reed, and all for thee.
Dost thou hear me?　Art a god, Apollo?
Tell me then—a man whose purse is hollow,
Will find the wherewithal to fill it—where? "

PETRONIUS ARBITER

SOMNIA, quae mentes ludunt volitantibus umbris,
non delubra deum nec ab æthere numina mittunt,
sed sibi quisque facit. nam cum prostrata sopore
urget membra quies et mens sine pondere ludit,
quidquid luce fuit tenebris agit. oppida bello
qui quatit et flammis miserandas eruit urbes,
tela videt versasque acies et funera regum
atque exundantes profuso sanguine campos.
qui causas orare solent, legesque forumque
et pavidi cernunt inclusum chorte tribunal.
condit avarus opes defossumque invenit aurum.
venator saltus canibus quatit. eripit undis
aut premit eversam periturus navita puppem.
scribit amatori meretrix, dat adultera munus:
et canis in somnis leporis vestigia lustrat.
in noctis spatium miserorum vulnera durant.

PETRONIUS ARBITER

DREAMS, dreams that mock us with their flitting shadows,
They come not from the temples of the gods,
They send them not, the powers of the air.
Each man makes his own dreams. The body lies
Quiet in sleep, what time the mind set free
Follows in darkness what it sought by day.
He who makes kingdoms quake for fear and sends
Unhappy cities ruining in fire,
Sees hurtling blows and broken fighting ranks
And death of kings and sodden battle fields.
The lawyer sees the judge, the crowded court,
The miser hides his coin, digs buried treasure,
The hunter shakes the forests with his hounds,
The sailor rescues from the sea his ship,
Or drowning, clings to it. Mistress to lover
Writes a love-letter: the adulteress
Yields in her sleep, and in his sleep the hound
Is hot upon the traces of the hare.
The wounds of the unhappy in the night
Do but prolong their pain.

PETRONIUS ARBITER

Qualis nox fuit illa, di deaeque,
quam mollis torus. haesimus calentes
et transfudimus hinc et hinc labellis
errantes animas. valete, curae
mortales.

MS. OF ST. RÉMY AT RHEIMS

Pulchra comis annisque decens et candida vultu
 dulce quiescenti basia blanda dabas.
si te iam vigilans non unquam cernere possum,
 somne, precor, iugiter lumina nostra tene.

PETRONIUS ARBITER

Ah God, ah God, that night when we two clung
So close, our hungry lips
Transfused each into each our hovering souls,
Mortality's eclipse!

MS. OF ST. RÉMY AT RHEIMS

Young and gold-haired, fair of face,
  Thou gav'st me tender kisses in my sleep.
If waking I may never look upon thee,
  O Sleep, I pray you, never let me wake!

MS. OF BEAUVAIS

TE vigilans oculis, animo te nocte requiro,
  victa iacent solo cum mea membra toro.
vidi ego me tecum falsa sub imagine somni.
  somnia tu vinces, si mihi vera venis.

MS. OF BEAUVAIS

O BLANDOS oculos et inquietos
et quadam propria nota loquaces!
illic et Venus et leves Amores
atque ipsa in medio sedet Voluptas.

MS. OF BEAUVAIS

By day mine eyes, by night my soul desires thee,
    Weary, I lie alone.
Once in a dream it seemed thou wert beside me;
  O far beyond all dreams, if thou wouldst come!

MS. OF BEAUVAIS

O LOVELY restless eyes, that speak
    In language's despite!
For there sits Beauty, and the little Loves:
    Between them dwells Delight.

CODEX SALMASIANUS

Dic quid agis, formosa Venus, si nescis amanti
ferre vicem? perit omne decus, dum deperit aetas.
marcent post rorem violae, rosa perdit odorem,
lilia post vernum posito candore liquescunt.
haec metuas exempla precor, et semper amanti
redde vicem, quia semper amat, qui semper amatur.

CODEX SALMASIANUS

LOVELY Venus, what's to do
If the loved loves not again?
Beauty passes, youth's undone,
Violets wither, 'spite of dew,
Roses shrivel in the sun,
Lilies all their whiteness stain.
Lady, take these home to you,
And who loves thee, love again.

AUSONIUS

De rosis nascentibus

VER erat et blando mordentia frigora sensu
   spirabat croceo mane revecta dies
strictior Eoos praecesserat aura iugales,
   aestiferum suadens anticipare diem.
errabam riguis per quadrua compita in hortis,
   maturo cupiens me vegetare die.
vidi concretas per gramina flexa pruinas
   pendere aut holerum stare cacuminibus
caulibus et patulis teretes conludere guttas.

    .   .   .   .   .

vidi Paestano gaudere rosaria cultu
   exoriente novo roscida Lucifero
rara pruinosis canebat gemma frutetis
   ad primi radios interitura die
ambigeres, raperetne rosis Aurora ruborem
   an daret et flores tingeret orta dies
ros unus, color unus, et unum mane duorum
   sideris et floris nam domina una Venus
forsan et unus odor: sed celsior ille per auras
   difflatur, spirat proximus iste magis.
communis Paphie dea sideris et dea floris
   praecipit unius muricis esse habitum
momentum intererat, quo se nascentia florum
   germina comparibus dividerent spatiis.

AUSONIUS

On newblown roses

SPRING, and the sharpness of the golden dawn.
Before the sun was up a cooler breeze
Had blown, in promise of a day of heat,
And I was walking in my formal garden,
To freshen me, before the day grew old.

I saw the hoar frost stiff on the bent grasses,
Sitting in fat globes on the cabbage leaves,
And all my Paestum roses laughing at me,
Dew-drenched, and in the East the morning star,
And here and there a dewdrop glistening white,
That soon must perish in the early sun.

Think you, did Dawn steal colour from the roses,
Or was it new born day that stained the rose?
To each one dew, one crimson, and one morning,
To star and rose, their lady Venus one.
Mayhap one fragrance, but the sweet of Dawn
Drifts through the sky, and closer breathes the rose.

A moment dies: this bud that was new born
Has burgeoned even fold on even fold;
This still is green, with her close cap of leaves,
This shows a red stain on her tender sheath,
This the first crimson of the loosened bud;

haec viret angusto foliorum tecta galero,
  hanc tenui folio purpura rubra notat,
haec aperit primi fastigia celsa obelisci,
  mucronem absolvens purpurei capitis.
vertice collectos illa exsinuabat amictus
  iam meditans foliis se numerare suis.
nec mora: ridentis calathi patefecit honorem
  prodens inclusi semina densa croci.
haec modo, quae toto rutilaverat igne comarum,
  pallida collapsis deseritur foliis.
mirabar celerem fugitiva aetate rapinam
  et dum nascentur consenuisse rosas.
ecce et defluxit rutili coma punica floris,
  dum loquor, et tellus tecta rubore micat.
tot species, tantosque ortus variosque novatus
  una dies aperit, conficit ipsa dies.
conquerimur, Natura, brevis quod gratia florum est.
  ostentata oculis ilico dona rapis.
quam longa una dies, aetas tam longa rosarum,
  quas pubescentes iuncta senecta premit.
quam modo nascentem rutilus conspexit Eous,
  hanc rediens sero vespere vidit anum.
sed bene quod paucis licet interitura diebus
  succedens aevum prorogat ipsa suum.
collige, virgo, rosas, dum flos novus et nova pubes,
  et memor esto aevum sic properare tuum.

And now she thinks to unwind her coverings,
And lo! the glory of the radiant chalice,
Scatt'ring the close seeds of her golden heart.
One moment, all on fire and crimson glowing,
All pallid now and bare and desolate.
I marvelled at the flying rape of time;
But now a rose was born: that rose is old.
Even as I speak the crimson petals float
Down drifting, and the crimsoned earth is bright.

So many lovely things, so rare, so young,
A day begat them, and a day will end.
O Earth, to give a flower so brief a grace!
As long as a day is long, so long the life of a rose.
The golden sun at morning sees her born,
And late at eve returning finds her old.
Yet wise is she, that hath so soon to die,
And lives her life in some succeeding rose.
O maid, while youth is with the rose and thee,
Pluck thou the rose: life is as swift for thee.

AUSONIUS

Mosella

Quis color ille vadis, seras cum propulit umbras
Hesperus et viridi perfudit monte Mosellam!
tota natant crispis iuga motibus et tremit absens
pampinus et vitreis vindemia turget in undis.

AUSONIUS

Silva Myrtea

Errantes silva in magna et sub luce maligna
inter harundineasque comas gravidumque papaver
et tacitos sine labe lacus, sine murmure rivos,
quorum per ripas nebuloso lumine marcent
fleti, olim regum et puerorum nomina, flores.

AUSONIUS

Evening on the Moselle

WHAT colour are they now, thy quiet waters?
The evening star has brought the evening light,
And filled the river with the green hillside;
The hill-tops waver in the rippling water,
Trembles the absent vine and swells the grape
In thy clear crystal.

AUSONIUS

The Fields of Sorrow

THEY wander in deep woods, in mournful light,
Amid long reeds and drowsy headed poppies,
And lakes where no wave laps, and voiceless streams,
Upon whose banks in the dim light grow old
Flowers that were once bewailèd names of kings.

AUSONIUS

Ad Uxorem

Uxor vivamus ut viximus et teneamus
   nomina quae primo sumpsimus in thalamo;
nec ferat ulla dies, ut commutemur in aevo,
   quin tibi sim iuvenis tuque puella mihi.
Nestore sim quamvis provectior aemulaque annis
   vincas Cumanam tu quoque Deiphoben,
nos ignoremus quid sit matura senectus,
   scire aevi meritum, non numerare decet.

AUSONIUS

To his Wife

LOVE, let us live as we have lived, nor lose
   The little names that were the first night's grace,
And never come the day that sees us old,
   I still your lad, and you my little lass.
Let me be older than old Nestor's years,
   And you the Sibyl, if we heed it not.
What should we know, we two, of ripe old age?
   We'll have its richness, and the years forgot.

PAULINUS OF NOLA

Ad Ausonium

Non inopes animi neque de feritate legentes
desertis habitare locis, sed in ardua versi
sidera spectantesque deum verique profunda
perspicere intenti, de vanis libera curis
otia amant strepitumque fori rerumque tumultus
cunctaque divinis inimica negotia donis
et Christi imperiis et amore salutis abhorrent
speque fideque deum sponsa mercede sequuntur,
quam referet certus non desperantibus auctor,
si modo non vincant vacuis praesentia rebus,
quaeque videt spernat, quae non videt ut mereatur
secreta ignitus penetrans caelestia sensus.
namque caduca patent nostris, aeterna negantur
visibus, et nunc spe sequimur quod mente videmus.
spernentes varias, rerum spectacula, formas
et male corporeos bona sollicitantia visus.
attamen haec sedisse illis sententia visa est,
tota quibus iam lux patuit verique bonique,
venturi aeternum saecli et praesentis inane.

PAULINUS OF NOLA

To Ausonius

Not that they beggared be in mind, or brutes,
That they have chosen their dwelling place afar
In lonely places: but their eyes are turned
To the high stars, the very deep of Truth.
Freedom they seek, an emptiness apart
From worthless hopes: din of the marketplace,
And all the noisy crowding up of things,
And whatsoever wars on the divine,
At Christ's command and for His love, they hate;
By faith and hope they follow after God,
And know their quest shall not be desperate,
If but the Present conquer not their souls
With hollow things: that which they see they spurn
That they may come at what they do not see,
Their senses kindled like a torch, that may
Blaze through the secrets of eternity.
The transient's open, everlastingness
Denied our sight; yet still by hope we follow
The vision that our minds have seen, despising
The shows and forms of things, the loveliness
Soliciting for ill our mortal eyes.
The present's nothing: but eternity
Abides for those on whom all truth, all good,
Hath shone, in one entire and perfect light.

PAULINUS OF NOLA

Ad Ausonium

EGO te per omne quod datum mortalibus
    et destinatum saeculum est
claudente donec continebor corpore,
    discernar orbe quolibet,
nec ore longe, nec remotum lumine
    tenebo fibris insitum,
videbo corde, mente complectar pia,
    ubique praesentem mihi.
et cum solutus corporali carcere,
    terraque provolavero,
quo me locarit axe communis Pater,
    illic quoque animo te geram.
neque finis idem, qui meo me corpore,
    et amore laxabit tuo,
mens quippe, lapsis quae superstes artubus,
    de stirpe durat caeliti,
sensus necesse est simul et affectus suos
    retineat ut vitam suam;
et ut mori sic oblivisci non capit,
    perenne vivax et memor.

PAULINUS OF NOLA

To Ausonius

I, THROUGH all chances that are given to mortals,
   And through all fates that be,
So long as this close prison shall contain me,
   Yea, though a world shall sunder me and thee,

Thee shall I hold, in every fibre woven,
   Not with dumb lips, nor with averted face
Shall I behold thee, in my mind embrace thee,
   Instant and present, thou, in every place.

Yea, when the prison of this flesh is broken,
   And from the earth I shall have gone my way,
Wheresoe'er in the wide universe I stay me,
   There shall I bear thee, as I do to-day.

Think not the end, that from my body frees me,
   Breaks and unshackles from my love to thee;
Triumphs the soul above its house in ruin,
   Deathless, begot of immortality.

Still must she keep her senses and affections,
   Hold them as dear as life itself to be.
Could she choose death, then might she choose forgetting:
   Living, remembering, to eternity.

PAULINUS OF NOLA

Carmen in S. Felicem

VER avibus voces aperit, mea lingua suum ver
natalem Felicis habet, quo lumine et ipsa
floret hiems populis gaudentibus; et licet atro
frigore tempus adhuc mediis hiberna pruinis
ducat, concretum terris canentibus annum,
ista luce tamen nobis pia gaudia laetum
ver faciunt. cedit pulsis a pectore curis
maeror, hiems animi; fugiunt a corde sereno
nubila tristitiae. sicut cognoscit amicos
mitis hirundo dies et pinnis candida nigris
ales et illa piae turtur cognata columbae,
nec nisi vere novo resonant acalanthida dumi,
quaeque sub hirsutis mutae modo saepibus errant
mox reduci passim laetantur vere volucres,
tam variae linguis quam versicoloribus alis:
sic et ego agnosco diem, quem sancta quotannis
festa novant iusto magni Felicis honore.
nunc placidum mihi ver gaudente renascitur anno,
nunc libet ora modis et carmina solvere votis
vocibus et vernare novis.

PAULINUS OF NOLA

For St. Felix' Day

SPRING wakens the birds' voices, but for me
My Saint's day is my spring, and in its light
For all his happy folk the winter flowers.
Keen frost without, midwinter, and the year
Rigid with cold and all the country white,
But gone the harder winter of the soul.

Even as the gentle swallow knows the days
That are his friends, the white bird with black wings,
And the kind turtle-doves, and no bird sings,
But silently slips through the ragged copses,
Till the day comes that the thorn trees are loud
With the greenfinches, then what shining wings
And what gay voices, so I know the day
Year after year that is St. Felix' Feast,
And know the springtime of my year is come,
And sing him a new song.

PAULINUS OF NOLA

Verbum crucis

CERNE deum nostro velatum corpore Christum,
qui fragilis carne est, verbo cibus et cruce amarus:
dura superficies, verbum crucis et crucis esca est,
coelestem Christi claudens in carne medullam.
sed cruce dulcis item, quia protulit arbore vitam
vita deus noster; ligno mea vita pependit,
ut staret mea vita deo. quid, vita, rependam
pro vita tibi, Christe, mea? nisi forte salutis
accipiam calicem, quo me tua dextra propinet,
ut sacro mortis pretiosae proluar haustu.
sed quid agam? neque si proprium dem corpus in ignes
vilescamque mihi, nec sanguine debita fuso
iusta tibi solvam, quia me reddam tibi pro me,
et quicquid simili vice fecero, semper ero impar,
Christe, tibi, quia tu pro me mea, non tua, Christe,
debita soluisti, pro servis passus iniquis.
quis tibi penset amor? dominus mea forma fuisti,
ut servus tua forma forem; et res magna putatur
mercari propriam de re pereunte salutem?
perpetuis mutare caduca et vendere terram,
caelum emere? ecce deus quanto me carius emit
morte crucis? passus, deiectus imagine servi,
ut viles emeret pretioso sanguine servos.

PAULINUS OF NOLA

The Word of the Cross

Look on thy God, Christ hidden in our flesh.
A bitter word, the cross, and bitter sight:
Hard rind without, to hold the heart of heaven.
Yet sweet it is; for God upon that tree
Did offer up His life: upon that rood
My Life hung, that my life might stand in God.
Christ, what am I to give Thee for my life?
Unless take from Thy hands the cup they hold,
To cleanse me with the precious draught of death.
What shall I do? My body to be burned?
Make myself vile? The debt's not paid out yet.
Whate'er I do, it is but I and Thou,
And still do I come short, still must Thou pay
My debts, O Christ; for debts Thyself hadst none.
What love may balance Thine? My Lord was found
In fashion like a slave, that so His slave
Might find himself in fashion like his Lord.
Think you the bargain's hard, to have exchanged
The transient for the eternal, to have sold
Earth to buy Heaven? More dearly God bought me.

PRUDENTIUS

Hymnus ante somnum

FLUXIT labor diei,
  redit et quietis hora,
blandus sopor vicissim
  fessos relaxat artus.

mens aestuans procellis
  curisque sauciata
totis bibit medullis
  obliviale poclum.

serpit per omne corpus
  Lethea vis, nec ullum
miseris doloris aegri
  patitur manere sensum. . . .

corpus licet fatiscens
  jaceat recline paullum,
Christum tamen sub ipso
  meditabimur sopore.

PRUDENTIUS

Before Sleep

THE toil of day is ebbing,
   The quiet comes again,
In slumber deep relaxing
   The limbs of tired men.

And minds with anguish shaken,
   And spirits racked with grief,
The cup of all forgetting
   Have drunk and found relief.

The still Lethean waters
   Now steal through every vein,
And men no more remember
   The meaning of their pain. . . .

Let, let the weary body
   Lie sunk in slumber deep.
The heart shall still remember
   Christ in its very sleep.

PRUDENTIUS

Hymnus circa Exsequias Defuncti

Nunc suscipe, terra, fovendum,
  gremioque hunc concipe molli.
hominis tibi membra sequestro,
  generosa et fragmina credo.

animae fuit haec domus olim,
  factoris ab ore creatae;
fervens habitavit in istis
  sapientia principe Christo.

tu depositum tege corpus;
  non immemor ille requiret
sua munera factoi et auctor
  propriique aenigmata vultus.

veniant modo tempora justa
  cum spem Deus impleat omnem,
reddas patefacta, necesse est,
  qualem tibi trado figuram.

non si cariosa vetustas
  dissolverit ossa favillis
fueritque cinisculus arens
  minimi mensura pugilli,

nec si vaga flamina et aurae
  vacuum per inane volantes
tulerint cum pulvere nervos
  hominem periisse licebit.

PRUDENTIUS

The Burial of the Dead

TAKE him, earth, for cherishing,
  To thy tender breast receive him.
Body of a man I bring thee,
  Noble even in its ruin.

Once was this a spirit's dwelling,
  By the breath of God created.
High the heart that here was beating,
  Christ the prince of all its living.

Guard him well, the dead I give thee,
  Not unmindful of His creature
Shall He ask it: He who made it
  Symbol of His mystery.

Comes the hour God hath appointed
  To fulfil the hope of men,
Then must thou, in very fashion,
  What I give, return again.

Not though ancient time decaying
  Wear away these bones to sand,
Ashes that a man might measure
  In the hollow of his hand:

Not though wandering winds and idle,
  Drifting through the empty sky,
Scatter dust was nerve and sinew,
  Is it given man to die.

patet ecce fidelibus ampli
   via lucida iam paradisi.
licet et nemus illud adire
   homini quod ademerat anguis.

illic, precor, optime ductor,
   famulam tibi praecipe mentem,
genitali in sede sacrari
   quam liquerat exsul et errans.

nos tecta fovebimus ossa
   violis et fronde frequenti
titulumque et frigida saxa
   liquido spargemus odore.

Once again the shining road
   Leads to ample Paradise;
Open are the woods again
   That the Serpent lost for men.

Take, O take him, mighty Leader,
   Take again thy servant's soul,
To the house from which he wandered
   Exiled, erring, long ago.

But for us, hap earth about him,
   Earth with leaves and violets strewn,
Grave his name, and pour the fragrant
   Balm upon the icy stone.

BOETHIUS

Quaenam discors foedera rerum
causa resoluit? quis tanta deus
veris statuit bella duobus,
ut quae carptim singula constent
eadem nolint mixta iugari?
an discordia nulla est veris
semperque sibi certa cohaerent?
sed mens caecis obruta membris
nequit oppressi luminis igne
rerum tenues noscere nexus.
sed cur tanto flagrat amore
veri tectas reperire notas?
scitne quod appetit anxia nosse?
sed quis nota scire laborat?
at si nescit, quid caeca petit?
quis enim quidquam nescius optet
aut quis valeat nescita sequi?
quove inveniat, quisve repertam
queat ignarus noscere formam?
an cum mentem cerneret altam
pariter summam et singula norat?
nunc membrorum condita nube
non in totum est oblita sui
summamque tenet singula perdens.
igitur quisquis vera requirit

BOETHIUS

THIS discord in the pact of things,
This endless war twixt truth and truth,
That singly hold, yet give the lie
To him who seeks to yoke them both—
Do the gods know the reason why?

Or is truth one without a flaw,
And all things to each other turn,
But the soul, sunken in desire,
No longer can the links discern,
In glimmering of her smothered fire?

Then why with travail does she yearn
To find the hidden mysteries?
Knows she the thing for which she burns?
Yet who will seek what he hath got?
Yet who will seek he knows not what?

How shall he follow the unknown?
How shall he find it, and when found
How shall he know it?   Did the soul
Once see the universal mind,
And know the part, and know the whole?

Now sunken in the mirk of sense,
Not wholly doth the soul forget,
Still grasps the whole, lets go the part:
And therefore whoso seeks the truth
Shall find in no wise peace of heart.

neutro est habitu: nam neque novit
nec penitus tamen omnia nescit:
sed quam retinens meminit summam
consulit alte visa retractans,
ut servatis queat oblitas
addere partes.

For neither doth he wholly know,
And neither doth he all forget:
But that high thing which once he saw,
And still remembers, that he holds,
And seeks to bring the truth forgot
Again to that which he hath yet.

BOETHIUS

Stupet tergeminus novo
captus carmine ianitor,   30
quae sontes agitant metu
ultrices scelerum deae
iam maestae lacrimis madent.
non ixionium caput
velox praecipitat rota,
et longa site perditus
spernit flumina Tantalus.
vultur dum satur est modis,
non trahit Tityi iecur.
tandem " vincimur " arbiter   40
umbrarum miserans ait :
" donamus comitem viro
emptam carmine coniugem.
sed lex dona coerceat,
ne, dum Tartara liquerit,
fas sit lumina flectere."
quis legem dat amantibus ?
maior lex amor est sibi.
heu noctis prope terminos
Orpheus Eurydicen suam   50
vidit perdidit occidit.
vos haec fabula respicit
quicumque in superum diem
mentem ducere quaeritis.
nam qui tartareum in specus
victus lumina flexerit,
quidquid praecipuum trahit
perdit, dum videt inferos.

BOETHIUS

CERBERUS at Hell's gate was still,
    Dazed captive to an unknown song:
No longer plunged the turning wheel,
    And Tantalus, athirst so long,

Heeded the streams no more: the three
    Avenging goddesses of ill
Wept, sad at heart; of melody
    The very vulture drank his fill.

" Yea, thou hast conquered," said the Lord
    Of Shadows, " Take her, but be wise.
Thy song hath bought her, but on her
    Turn not, this side of Hell, thine eyes."

Yet is not Love his greater law?
    And who for lovers shall decree?
On the sheer threshold of the night
    Orpheus saw Eurydice.

Looked, and destroyed her.   Ye who read,
    Look up: the gods in daylight dwell.
All that you hold of loveliness
    Sinks from you, looking down at Hell.

BOETHIUS

Si vis celsi iura tonantis
pura sollers cernere mente,
aspice summi culmina caeli.
illic iusto foedere rerum
veterem servant sidera pacem.
non sol rutilo concitus igne
gelidum Phoebes impedit axem
nec quae summo vertice mundi
flectit rapidos ursa meatus
numquam occiduo lota profundo
cetera cernens sidera mergi
cupit oceano tinguere flammas.
semper vicibus temporis aequis
Vesper seras nuntiat umbras
revehitque diem Lucifer almum.
sic aeternos reficit cursus
alternus amor, sic astrigeris
bellum discors exulat oris.

BOETHIUS

Iғ the high counsels of the Lord of Thunder
Seekest thou to know with singleness of heart,
Look to the highest of the heights of heaven,
See where the stars still keep their ancient peace.
    Never the kindled fiery sun
    Hinders the gliding frozen moon,
    Nor halts on his high way the Bear,
    Nor in the west where waters are,
    And where the other stars go down,
    Seeks he his silver flames to drown.
    With even alternate return
    Still Vesper brings the evening on,
    And Lucifer the tender dawn.
    So Love still guides their deathless ways,
    And ugly Hate that maketh wars
    Is exiled from the shore of stars.

BOETHIUS

ITE nunc fortes ubi celsa magni
ducit exempli via.   cur inertes
terga nudatis?   superata tellus
sidera donat.

BOETHIUS

O STRONG of heart, go where the road
Of ancient honour climbs.
Bow not your craven shoulders.
Earth conquered gives the stars.

VENANTIUS FORTUNATAS

Ad domnam Radigundem

TEMPORA si solito mihi candida lilia ferrent
   aut speciosa foret suave rubore rosa,
haec ego rure legens aut caespite pauperis horti
   misissem magnis munera parva libens.
sed quia prima mihi desunt, vel solvo secunda:
   profert qui vicias ferret amore rosas.
inter odoriferas tamen has quas misimus herbas
   purpureae violae nobile germen habent.
respirant pariter regali murice tinctae
   et saturat foliis hinc odor, inde decor.
hae quod utrumque gerunt pariter habeatis utraque,
   et sit mercis odor flore perenne decus.

VENANTIUS FORTUNATUS

To the Lady Radegunde, with Violets

IF 'twere the time of lilies,
    Or of the crimson rose,
I'd pluck them in the fields for you,
    Or my poor garden close:
Small gift for you so rare.

But I can find no lilies,
    Green herbs are all I bring.
Yet love makes vetches roses,
    And in their shadowing
Hide violets as fair.

For royal is their purple,
    And fragrant is their breath,
And to one sweet and royal,
    Their fragrance witnesseth
Beauty abiding there.

VENANTIUS FORTUNATUS

Item ad eandem pro floribus transmissis

O REGINA potens, aurum cui et purpura vile est,
    floribus ex parvis te veneratur amans.
et si non res est, color est tamen ipse per herbas:
    purpura per violas, aurea forma crocus.
dives amore dei vitasti praemia mundi:
    illas contemnens has retinebis opes.
suscipe missa tibi variorum munera florum,
    ad quos te potius vita beata vocat.
quae modo te crucias, recreanda in luce futura,
    aspicis hinc qualis te retinebit ager.
per ramos fragiles quos nunc praebemus olentes
    perpende hinc quantus te refovebit odor.
haec cui debentur precor ut, cum veneris illuc,
    meque tuis meritis dextera blanda trahat.
quamvis te exspectet paradisi gratia florum,
    isti vos cupiunt iam revidere foris.
et licet egregio videantur odore placere,
    plus ornant proprias te redeunte comas.

VENANTIUS FORTUNATUS

To the Lady Radegunde with a Bunch of Flowers

O QUEEN, that art so high
　Purple and gold thou passest by,
With these poor flowers thy lover worships thee.
Though all thy wealth thou hast flung far from thee,
　　Wilt thou not hold
　The violet's purple and the crocus' gold?

　Take this poor offering,
　For it thy thoughts shall bring
To that blest light that is to dawn for thee,
　　Fields bright as these,
　And richer fragrances.

　And when thou comest there,
　Hear, O my Saint, my prayer,
And may thy kind hand draw me after thee.
　　Yet, though thine eyes
　Already look on flowers of Paradise,

　These thine own flowers
　Would have thee out of doors.
Yea, though the flowers of Paradise are sweet,
　　These fain would lie
　Where thou wert passing by.

VENANTIUS FORTUNATUS

Ad Rucconem diaconum, modo presbyterum

ALTARIS domini pollens, bone Rucco, minister,
    hinc tibi festinus mando salutis opus.
nos maris Oceani tumidum circumfluit aequor,
    te quoque Parisius, care sodalis, habet;
Sequana te retinet, nos unda Britannica cingit:
    divisis terris alligat unus amor.
non furor hic pelagi vultum mihi subtrahit illum
    nec boreas aufert nomen, amice, tuum.
pectore sub nostro tam saepe recurris amator,
    tempore sub hiemis quam solet unda maris.
ut quatitur pelagus quotiens proflaverit eurus,
    stat neque sic animus te sine, care, meus.

VENANTIUS FORTUNATUS

Written on an island off the Breton coast

You at God's altar stand, His minister,
  And Paris lies about you and the Seine:
Around this Breton isle the Ocean swells,
  Deep water and one love between us twain.

Wild is the wind, but still thy name is spoken;
  Rough is the sea: it sweeps not o'er thy face.
Still runs my love for shelter to its dwelling,
  Hither, O heart, to thine abiding place

Swift as the waves beneath an east wind breaking
  Dark as beneath a winter sky the sea,
So to my heart crowd memories awaking,
  So dark, O love, my spirit without thee.

VENANTIUS FORTUNATUS

Ad Gogonem cum me rogaret ad cenam

NECTAR vina cibus vestis doctrina facultas—
    muneribus largis tu mihi, Gogo, sat es;
tu refluus Cicero, tu noster Apicius extas,
    hinc satias verbis, pascis et inde cibis.
sed modo da veniam; bubla turgente quiesco,
    nam fit lis uteri, si caro mixta fremat.
hic ubi bos recubat, fugiet puto pullus et anser
    cornibus et pinnis non furor aequus erit.
et modo iam somno languentia lumina claudo;
    nam dormire meum carmina lenta probant.

VENANTIUS FORTUNATUS

To Gogo, that he can eat no more

NECTAR and wine and food and scholar's wit,
  Such is the fashion, Gogo, of thy house.
Cicero art thou, and Apicius too,
  But now I cry you mercy: no more goose!
Where the ox lieth, dare the chickens come?
  Nay, horn and wing unequal warfare keep.
My eyes are closing and my lute is dumb,
  Slower and slower go my songs to sleep.

VENANTIUS FORTUNATUS

Ad Iovinum inlustrem ac patricium et rectorem provinciae

TEMPORA lapsa volant, fugitivis fallimur horis . . .
   sic quoque dissimiles ad finem tendimus omnes,
     nemo pedem retrahit quo sibi limes erit . . .
quid sunt arma viris? cadit Hector et ultor Achilles,
     Aiax, in clipeo murus Achaeus, obit . . .
forma venusta fluit, cecidit pulcherrimus Astur,
     occubat Hippolytus nec superextat Adon.
quid, rogo, cantus agit? modulis blanditus acutis
     Orpheus et citharae vox animata iacet. . . .
quidve poema potest? Maro Naso Menander Homerus,
     quorum nuda tabo membra sepulchra tegunt?
cum venit extremum, neque Musis carmina prosunt,
     nec iuvat eloquio detinuisse melos.
sic, dum puncta cadunt, fugiunt praesentia rerum,
     et vitae tabulam tessera rapta levat. . . .
quod superest obitu meritorum flore beato,
     suavis iustorum fragrat odor tumulo.

VENANTIUS FORTUNATUS

TIME that is fallen is flying, we are fooled by the passing
      hours . . .
Likeness is none between us, but we go to the selfsame end.
The foot that hath crossed that threshold shall no man with-
      draw again.
. . . What help in the arms of the fighters? Hector, and
      vengeful Achilles
   Fallen, Ajax is fallen, whose shield was the wall of
      Greece.
Beauty, beauty passeth, Astur the fairest is fallen,
Low Hippolytus lieth, Adonis liveth no more.
And where are the songs of the singers? Silent for all their
      sweetness.
Orpheus and the voice of the lute that he wakened are still.
Yea, but the poets, Virgil, Ovid, Menander and Homer?
Their naked bones are laid in the damps of the grave.
Come to the end, small aid is there in the songs of the Muses.
Small joy to be won in prolonging the notes of the song.
Even as the moments are dying, the present is flying,
The dice are snatched from our hands and the game is done.
Naught but the deeds of the just live on in a flower that is
      blessèd;
Sweetness comes from the grave where a good man lieth
      dead.

ST. COLUMBA

Dies irae

Regis regum rectissimi
prope est dies domini,
dies irae et vindictae,
tenebrarum et nebulae,
diesque mirabilium
tonitruorum fortium,
dies quoque angustiae,
maeroris ac tristitiae,
in quo cessabit mulierum
amor et desiderium,
hominumque contentio
mundi huius et cupido.

ST. COLUMBA

The Day of Wrath

Day of the king most righteous,
   The day is nigh at hand,
The day of wrath and vengeance,
   And darkness on the land.

Day of thick clouds and voices,
   Of mighty thundering,
A day of narrow anguish
   And bitter sorrowing.

The love of women's over,
   And ended is desire,
Men's strife with men is quiet,
   And the world lusts no more.

A SCHOLAR OF MALMESBURY

Carmen Aldhelmo Datum

Ecce, nocturno tempore,
orto brumali turbine
quatiens terram tempestas
turbabat atque vastitas,
cum fracto venti federe
bacharentur in aethere
et rupto retinaculo
desevirent in saeculo. . . .
ac totidem torrentibus
septem latet lampadibus
Pliadis pulchra copula
ab Athlantis prosapia : . . .
Zodiacus cum cetera
cyclus fuscatur caterva,
quem Mazaroth reperimus
nuncupari antiquitus,
bis senis cum sideribus
per Olimpum lucentibus;
nec radiabat rutilus,
sicut solebat, Sirius,
quia nubis nigerrima
abscondunt polos pallia.
attamen flagrant fulmina
late per caeli culmina,
quando pallentem pendula
flammam vomunt fastigia,

A SCHOLAR OF MALMESBURY

To Aldhelm

STORM and destruction shattering
   Strike fear upon the world,
The winds are out, and through high heaven
   Their Bacchanals are hurled.
Their league is broken, burst the girth,
And launched their fury on the earth.

Torrent on torrent falls the rain,
   Dark are the lovely Pleiades,
Their seven lamps are out, and dark
   The Houses where abide the stars.
And Sirius shines no more at all,
And heaven is hung with blackest pall.

Yet through the summits of the sky
   Flashes afar the livid levin,
And cataracts of pallid fire
   Pour from the toppling crests of heaven.
Struggling with clouds the mountains stand,
The dark sea masses on the strand,
Following wave on wave behind
The rush and ruin of the wind.

quorum natura nubibus
procedit conlidentibus,
nec non marina cerula
glomerantur in glarea,
qua inruit inruptio
ventorum ac correptio.
per pelagi itinera
salsa spumabant equora,
cum bulliret brumalibus
undosus vortex fluctibus;
Oceanus cum motibus
atque diris dodrantibus
pulsabat promontoria
suffragante victoria.

Along the pathways of the sea
  The salt waves rise in foam.
The deep is boiling like a pot,
  Dark water seething furiously,
And Ocean with his might of war
And thunder of his waves afar,
Storming the headlands, shock on shock,
  And shouting victory.

COLMAN

Colmani Versus In Colmanum Perheriles Scottigena
Ficti Patrie Cupidum Et Remeantem

Dum subito properas dulces invisere terras
deseris et nostrae refugis consortia vitae,
festina citius, precibus nec flecteris ullis.
nec retinere valet blande suggestio vocis;
vincit amor patriae: quis flectere possit amantem?
nec sic arguerim deiectae tedia mentis;
nam mihi preterite Christus si tempora vitae,
et prisco iterum renovaret ab ordine vires,
si mihi quae quondam fuerat floresceret aetas
et nostros subito faceret nigrescere canos,
forsitan et nostram temptarent talia mentem;
tum modo da veniam pigreque ignosce senectae,
quae nimium nostris obstat nunc aemula votis.
audi doctiloquo cecinit quod carmine vates:
omnia fert aetas, gelidus tardante senecta
sanguis hebet, frigent effete in corpore vires.
siccae nec calido complentur sanguine venae.
me maris anfractus lustranda et littora terrent
et tu rumpe moras celeri sulcare carina.
Colmanique tui semper, Colmane, memento:
iamiam nunc liceat fida te voce monere.
pauca tibi dicam vigili que mente teneto:
non te pompiferi delectet gloria mundi,
quae volucri vento vanoque simillima somno
labitur et vacuas fertur ceu fumus in auras,

COLMAN

Written by Colman the Irishman to Colman returning to his own land

So, since your heart is set on those sweet fields
    And you must leave me here,
Swift be your going, heed not any prayers,
    Although the voice be dear.

Vanquished art thou by love of thine own land,
    And who shall hinder love?
Why should I blame thee for thy weariness,
    And try thy heart to move?

Since, if but Christ would give me back the past,
    And that first strength of days,
And this white head of mine were dark again,
    I too might go your ways.

Do but indulge an idle fond old man
    Whose years deny his heart.
The years take all away, the blood runs slow,
    No leaping pulses start.

All those far seas and shores that must be crossed,
    They terrify me: yet
Go thou, my son, swift be thy cleaving prow,
    And do not quite forget.

Hear me, my son; little have I to say.
    Let the world's pomp go by.
Swift is it as a wind, an idle dream,
    Smoke in an empty sky.

75

fluminis et validi cursu fluit ocior omni.
Vade libens patriae quoniam te cura remordet.
omnipotens genitor nostrae spes unica vitae
qui maris horrisonos fluctus ventosque gubernat
det tibi nunc tutas crispantis gurgitis undas.
ipse tuae liquidis rector sit navis in undis,
aequore nubiferi devectum flatibus auri
reddat ad optate scottorum littora terrae.
tunc valeas fame felix multosque per annos
vivas aegregiae capiens praeconia vitae.
hic ego praesentis nunc gaudia temporis opto,
ut tibi perpetuae contingant gaudia vitae.

Go to the land whose love gives thee no rest,
  And may Almighty God,
Hope of our life, lord of the sounding sea,
  Of winds and waters lord,

Give thee safe passage on the wrinkled sea,
  Himself thy pilot stand,
Bring thee through mist and foam to thy desire,
  Again to Irish land.

Live, and be famed and happy: all the praise
  Of honoured life to thee.
Yea, all this world can give thee of delight,
  And then eternity.

ALCUIN

Versus de Cuculo

Heu, cuculus nobis fuerat cantare suetus,
    quae te nunc rapuit hora nefanda tuis?
heu, cuculus, cuculus, qua te regione reliqui,
    infelix nobis illa dies fuerat.
omne genus hominum cuculum conplangat ubique,
    perditus est cuculus, heu, perit ecce meus.
non pereat cuculus, veniet sub tempore veris,
    et nobis veniens carmina laeta ciet.
quis scit, si veniat; timeo, est summersus in undis,
    vorticibus raptus atque necatus aquis.
heu mihi, si cuculum Bachus dimersit in undis,
    qui rapiet iuvenes vortice pestifero.
si vivat, redeat, nidosque recurrat ad almos,
    nec corvus cuculum dissecet ungue fero.
heu quis te, cuculus, nido rapit ecce paterno?
    heu, rapuit, rapuit, nescio si venias.
carmina si curas, cuculus, citus ecce venito,
    ecce venito, precor, ecce venito citus.
non tardare, precor, cuculus, dum currere possis,
    te Dafnis iuvenis optat habere tuus.
tempus adest veris, cuculus modo rumpe soporem,
    te cupit, en, senior atque Menalca pater.
en tondent nostri librorum prata iuvenci,
    solus abest cuculus, quis, rogo, pascit eum?
heu, male pascit eum Bachus, reor, impius ille,
    qui sub cuncta cupit vertere corda mala.

ALCUIN

Lament for the Cuckoo

O cuckoo that sang to us and art fled,
   Where'er thou wanderest, on whatever shore
Thou lingerest now, all men bewail thee dead,
   They say our cuckoo will return no more.
Ah, let him come again, he must not die,
   Let him return with the returning spring,
And waken all the songs he used to sing.
   But will he come again? I know not, I.

I fear the dark sea breaks above his head,
   Caught in the whirlpool, dead beneath the waves.
Sorrow for me, if that ill god of wine
   Hath drowned him deep where young things find their
     graves.
But if he lives yet, surely he will come,
   Back to the kindly nest, from the fierce crows.
Cuckoo, what took you from the nesting place?
   But will he come again? That no man knows.

If you love songs, cuckoo, then come again,
   Come again, come again, quick, pray you come.
Cuckoo, delay not, hasten thee home again,
   Daphnis who loveth thee longs for his own.
Now spring is here again, wake from thy sleeping,
   Alcuin the old man thinks long for thee.
Through the green meadows go the oxen grazing;
   Only the cuckoo is not. Where is he?

Plangite nunc cuculum, cuculum nunc plangite cuncti,
  ille recessit ovans, flens redit ille, puto.
opto tamen, flentem cuculum habeamus ut illum,
  et nos plangamus cum cuculo pariter.
plange tuos casus lacrimis, puer inclite, plange,
  et casus plangunt viscera tota tuos.
si non dura silex genuit te, plange, precamur,
  te memorans ipsum plangere forte potes.
dulcis amor nati cogit deflere parentem,
  natus ab amplexu dum rapitur subito.
dum frater fratrem germanum perdit amatum,
  quid nisi idem faciat, semper et ipse fleat.
tres olim fuimus, iunxit quos spiritus unus,
  vix duo nunc pariter, tertius ille fugit.
heu fugiet, fugiet, planctus quapropter amarus
  nunc nobis restat, carus abit cuculus.
carmina post illum mittamus, carmina luctus,
  carmina deducunt forte, reor, cuculum.
sis semper felix utinam, quocunque recedas,
  sis memor et nostri, semper ubique vale.

Wail for the cuckoo, everywhere bewail him,
   Joyous he left us: shall he grieving come?
Let him come grieving, if he will but come again,
   Yea, we shall weep with him, moan for his moan.
Unless a rock begat thee, thou wilt weep with us.
   How canst thou not, thyself remembering?
Shall not the father weep the son he lost him,
   Brother for brother still be sorrowing?

Once were we three, with but one heart among us.
   Scarce are we two, now that the third is fled.
Fled is he, fled is he, but the grief remaineth;
   Bitter the weeping, for so dear a head.
Send a song after him, send a song of sorrow,
   Songs bring the cuckoo home, or so they tell.
Yet be thou happy, wheresoe'er thou wanderest.
   Sometimes remember us.   Love, fare you well.

ALCUIN

Conflictus Veris et Hiemis

Conveniunt subito cuncti de montibus altis
pastores pecudum vernali luce sub umbra
arborea, pariter laetas celebrare Camenas.
adfuit et iuvenis Dafnis seniorque Palemon :
omnes hi cuculo laudes cantare parabant.
ver quoque florigero succinctus stemmate venit,
frigida venit Hiems, rigidis hirsuta capillis.
his certamen erat cuculi de carmine grande.
ver prior adlusit ternos modulamine versus.

Ver. Opto meus veniat cuculus, carissimus ales.
omnibus iste solet fieri gratissimus hospes
in tectis, modulans rutilo bona carmina rostro.

Hiems. *Tum glacialis Hiems respondit voce severa :*
non veniat cuculus, nigris sed dormiat antris.
iste famem secum semper portare suescit.

Ver. Opto meus veniat cuculus cum germine laeto,
frigora depellat, Phoebo comes almus in aevum,
Phoebus amat cuculum crescenti luce serena.

ALCUIN

The Strife between Winter and Spring

From the high mountains the shepherds came together,
Gathered in the spring light under branching trees,
Come to sing songs, Daphnis, old Palemon,
All making ready to sing the cuckoo's praises.
Thither came Spring, girdled with a garland,
Thither came Winter, with his shaggy hair.
Great strife between them on the cuckoo's singing.

Spring. I would that he were here,
    Cuckoo!
 Of all winged things most dear,
 To every roof the most beloved guest.
 Bright-billed, good songs he sings.

Winter. Let him not come,
    Cuckoo!
 Stay on in the dark cavern where he sleeps,
 For Hunger is the company he brings.

Spring. I would that he were here,
    Cuckoo!
 Gay buds come with him, and the frost is gone,
 Cuckoo, the age-long comrade of the sun.
 The days are longer and the light serene.

Hiems.   Non veniat cuculus, generat quia forte labores,
proelia congeminat, requiem disiungit amatam,
omnia disturbat; pelagi terraeque laborant.

Ver.   Quid tu, tarda Hiems, cuculo convitia cantas?
qui torpore gravi tenebrosis tectus in antris
post epulas Veneris, post stulti pocula Bacchi.

Hiems.   Sunt mihi divitiae, sunt et convivia laeta,
est requies dulcis, calidus est ignis in aede.
haec cuculus nescit, sed perfidus ille laborat.

Ver.   Ore ferat flores cuculus, et mella ministrat,
aedificatque domus, placidas et navigat undas,
et generat soboles, laetos et vestiet agros.

Hiems.   Haec inimica mihi sunt, quae tibi laeta videntur.
sed placet optatas gazas numerare per arcas
et gaudere cibis simul et requiescere semper.

Ver.   Quis tibi, tarda Hiems, semper dormire parata,
divitias cumulat, gazas vel congregat ullas,
si ver vel aestas ante tibi nulla laborant?

Hiems.   Vera refers: illi, quoniam mihi multa laborant,
sunt etiam servi nostra ditione subacti.
iam mihi servantes domino, quaecumque laborant.

Ver.   Non illis dominus, sed pauper inopsque superbus.
nec te iam poteris per te tu pascere tantum
ni tibi qui veniet cuculus alimonia praestat.

Winter. Let him not come,
              Cuckoo!
  For toil comes with him and he wakens wars,
  Breaks blessed quiet and disturbs the world,
  And sea and earth alike sets travailing.

Spring. And what are you that throw your blame on him?
  That huddle sluggish in your half-lit caves
  After your feasts of Venus, bouts of Bacchus?

Winter. Riches are mine and joy of revelling,
  And sweet is sleep, the fire on the hearth stone.
  Nothing of these he knows, and does his treasons.

Spring. Nay, but he brings the flowers in his bright bill,
  And he brings honey, nests are built for him.
  The sea is quiet for his journeying,
  Young ones begotten, and the fields are green.

Winter. I like not these things which are joy to you.
  I like to count the gold heaped in my chests;
  And feast, and then to sleep, and then to sleep.

Spring. And who, thou slug-a-bed, got thee thy wealth?
  And who would pile thee any wealth at all,
  If spring and summer did not toil for thee?

Winter. Thou speakest truth; indeed they toil for me.
  They are my slaves, and under my dominion.
  As servants for their lord, they sweat for me.

Spring. No lord, but poor and beggarly and proud.
  Thou couldst not feed thyself a single day
  But for his charity who comes, who comes!
            Cuckoo!

Palemon. Tunc respondit ovans sublimi e sede Palemon
    et Dafnis pariter, pastorum et turba piorum :
    " Desine plura, Hiems : rerum tu prodigus, atrox.
    et veniat cuculus, pastorum dulcis amicus,
    collibus in nostris erumpant germina laeta,
    pascua sint pecori, requies et dulcis in arvis.
    et virides rami praestent umbracula fessis,
    uberibus plenis veniantque ad mulctra capellae,
    et volucres varia Phoebum sub voce salutent.
    quapropter citius cuculus nunc ecce venito!
    tu iam dulcis amor, cunctis gratissimus hospes.
    omnia te expectant, pelagus tellusque polusque.
    salve, dulce decus, cuculus per saecula salve! "

Then old Palemon spake from his high seat,
And Daphnis, and the crowd of faithful shepherds.
" Have done, have done, Winter, spendthrift and foul,
And let the shepherd's friend, the cuckoo, come.
And may the happy buds break on our hills,
Green be our grazing, peace in the ploughed fields,
Green branches give their shadow to tired men,
The goats come to the milking, udders full,
The birds call to the sun, each one his note.
Wherefore, O cuckoo, come, O cuckoo, come !
For thou art Love himself, the dearest guest,
And all things wait thee, sea and earth and sky.
All hail, beloved : through all ages, hail !

ALCUIN

De Luscinia

Quae te dextra mihi rapuit, luscinia, ruscis,
  illa meae fuerat invida laetitiae.
tu mea dulcisonis implesti pectora musis,
  atque animum moestum carmine mellifluo.
qua propter veniant volucrum simul undique coetus
  carmine te mecum plangere Pierio.
spreta colore tamen fueras non spreta canendo.
  lata sub angusto gutture vox sonuit,
dulce melos iterans vario modulamine Musae,
  atque creatorem semper in ore canens.
noctibus in furvis nusquam cessavit ab odis,
  vox veneranda sacris, o decus atque decor.
quid mirum, cherubim, seraphim si voce tonantem
  perpetua laudent, dum tua sic potuit?

ALCUIN

Written for his lost nightingale

WHOEVER stole you from that bush of broom,
 I think he envied me my happiness,
O little nightingale, for many a time
 You lightened my sad heart from its distress,
 And flooded my whole soul with melody.
And I would have the other birds all come,
 And sing along with me thy threnody.

So brown and dim that little body was,
 But none could scorn thy singing. In that throat
That tiny throat, what depth of harmony,
 And all night long ringing thy changing note.
 What marvel if the cherubim in heaven
Continually do praise Him, when to thee,
 O small and happy, such a grace was given?

ALCUIN

Sequentia de Sancto Michaele,
quam Alcuinus composuit Karolo imperatori

Summi regis archangele
Michahel,
intende, quaesumus, nostris
vocibus.

Te namque profitemur esse
supernorum principem civium.
te deum generi humano
orante diriguntur angeli,

Ne laedere inimici,
quantum cupiunt, versuti
fessos unquam mortales praevaleant.
idem tenes perpetui
potentiam paradisi,
semper te sancti honorant angeli.

In templo tu dei
turibulum aureum
visus es habuisse manibus.
inde scandens vapor
aromate plurimo
pervenit ante conspectum dei.

Tu crudelem cum draconem forti manu straveras,
faucibus illius animas eruisti plurimas.
hinc maximum agebatur in caelo silentium,
millia millium et dicunt " salus regi domino."

ALCUIN

A Sequence for St. Michael,
which Alcuin wrote for the Emperor Charles

MICHAEL, Archangel
Of the King of Kings,
Give ear to our voices.

We acknowledge thee to be the Prince of the citizens of
    heaven:
And at thy prayer God sends
His angels unto men,

That the enemy with cunning craft shall not prevail
To do the hurt he craves
To weary men.
Yea, thou hast the dominion of perpetual Paradise,
And ever do the holy angels honour thee.

Thou wert seen in the Temple of God,
A censer of gold in thy hands,
And the smoke of it fragrant with spices
Rose up till it came before God.

Thou with strong hand didst smite the cruel dragon,
And many souls didst rescue from his jaws.
Then was there a great silence in heaven,
And a thousand thousand saying " Glory to the Lord
    King."

Audi nos, Michahel,
angele summe,
huc parum descende
de poli sede,
nobis ferendo opem domini
levamen atque indulgentiae.

Tu nostros, Gabrihel,
hostes prosterne,
tu, Raphael, aegris
affer medelam,
morbos absterge, noxas minue,
nosque fac interesse gaudiis
beatorum.

Has tibi symphonias plectrat sophus, induperator.

Hear us, Michael,
Greatest angel,
Come down a little
From thy high seat,
To bring us the strength of God,
And the lightening of His mercy.

And do thou, Gabriel,
Lay low our foes,
And thou, Raphael,
Heal our sick,
Purge our disease, ease thou our pain,
And give us to share
In the joys of the blessed.

Emperor, thy scholar made these melodies for thee.

ALCUIN

Epitaphium

Hic, rogo, pauxillum veniens subsiste, viator,
    et mea scrutare pectore dicta tuo,
ut tua deque meis agnoscas fata figuris:
    vertitur o species, ut mea, sicque tua.
quod nunc es fueram, famosus in orbe, viator.
    et quod nunc ego sum, tuque futurus eris.
delicias mundi casso sectabar amore,
    nunc cinis et pulvis, vermibus atque cibus.
quapropter potius animam curare memento,
    quam carnem, quoniam haec manet, illa perit.
cur tibi rura paras? quam parvo cernis in antro
    me tenet hic requies: sic tua parva fiet.
cur Tyrio corpus inhias vestirier ostro
    quod mox esuriens pulvere vermis edet?
ut flores pereunt vento veniente minaci,
    sic tua namque, caro, gloria tota perit.
tu mihi redde vicem, lector, rogo, carminis huius
    et dic: " da veniam, Christe, tuo famulo."
obsecro, nulla manus violet pia iura sepulcri,
    personet angelica donec ab arce tuba:
" qui iaces in tumulo, terrae de pulvere surge,
    magnus adest iudex milibus innumeris."
Alchuine nomen erat sophiam mihi semper amanti,
    pro quo funde preces mente, legens titulum.

Hic requiescit beatae memoriae domnus Alchuinus abba,
qui obiit in pace xiv. kal. Iunias. quando legeritis, o vos
omnes, orate pro eo et dicite, " Requiem aeternam donet
ei dominus." Amen.

ALCUIN

His Epitaph

HERE halt, I pray you, make a little stay,
O wayfarer, to read what I have writ,
And know by my fate what thy fate shall be.
What thou art now, wayfarer, world-renowned,
I was: what I am now, so shall thou be.
The world's delight I followed with a heart
Unsatisfied: ashes am I, and dust.

Wherefore bethink thee rather of thy soul
Than of thy flesh;—this dieth, that abides.
Dost thou make wide thy fields? in this small house
Peace holds me now: no greater house for thee.
Wouldst have thy body clothed in royal red?
The worm is hungry for that body's meat.
Even as the flowers die in a cruel wind,
Even so, O flesh, shall perish all thy pride.

Now in thy turn, wayfarer, for this song
That I have made for thee, I pray you, say:
" Lord Christ, have mercy on Thy servant here,"
And may no hand disturb this sepulchre,
Until the trumpet rings from heaven's height,
" O thou that liest in the dust, arise,
The Judge of the unnumbered hosts is here! "

Alcuin was my name: learning I loved.
O thou that readest this, pray for my soul.

*Here lieth the Lord Abbot Alcuin of blessed memory, who died
in peace on the nineteenth of May. And when ye have read this,
do ye all pray for him and say, " May the Lord give him eternal
rest." Amen.*

95

FREDUGIS

Cella Alcuini

O MEA cella, mihi habitatio dulcis, amata,
    semper in aeternum, o mea cella, vale.
undique te cingit ramis resonantibus arbos,
    silvula florigeris semper onusta comis.
prata salutiferis florebunt omnia et herbis,
    quas medici quaerit dextra salutis ope.
flumina te cingunt florentibus undique ripis,
    retia piscator qua sua tendit ovans.
pomiferis redolent ramis tua claustra per hortos,
    lilia cum rosulis candida mixta rubris.
omne genus volucrum matutinas personat odas,
    atque creatorem laudat in ore deum.
in te personuit quondam vox alma magistri,
    quae sacro sophiae tradidit ore libros.
in te temporibus certis laus sancta tonantis
    pacificis sonuit vocibus atque animis.
te, mea cella, modo lacrimosis plango camenis,
    atque gemens casus pectore plango tuos.
tu subito quoniam fugisti carmina vatum,
    atque ignota manus te modo tota tenet.
te modo nec Flaccus nec vatis Homerus habebit,
    nec pueri musas per tua tecta canunt.
vertitur omne decus secli sic namque repente
    omnia mutantur ordinibus variis.

FREDUGIS

Lament for Alcuin

O LITTLE house, O dear and sweet my dwelling,
O little house, for ever fare thee well!
The trees stand round thee with their sighing branches,
A little flowering wood for ever fair,
A field in flower where one can gather herbs
To cure the sick;
Small streams about thee, all their banks in flower,
And there the happy fisher spreads his nets.
And all thy cloisters smell of apple orchards,
And there are lilies white and small red roses,
And every bird sings in the early morning,
Praising the God who made him in his singing.
And once the Master's kind voice sounded in thee,
Reading the books of old philosophy,
And at set times the holy hymn ascended
From hearts and voices both alike at peace.
O little house, my song is broke with weeping,
And sorrow is upon me for your end.
Silent the poets' songs, stilled in a moment,
And thou art passed beneath a stranger's hand.
No more shall Angilbert or Alcuin come,
Or the boys sing their songs beneath thy roof.
So passes all the beauty of the earth.

nil manet aeternum, nihil immutabile vere est.
  obscurat sacrum nox tenebrosa diem,
decutit et flores subito hiems frigida pulcros,
  perturbat placidum et tristior aura mare.
quae campis cervos agitabat sacra iuventus
  incumbit fessus nunc baculo senior.
nos miseri, cur te fugitivum, mundus, amamus?
  tu fugis a nobis semper ubique ruens.
tu fugiens fugias, Christum nos semper amemus,
  semper amor teneat pectora nostra dei.
ille pius famulos diro defendat ab hoste
  ad caelum rapiens pectora nostra, suos.
pectore quem pariter toto laudemus, amemus.
  nostra est ille pius gloria, vita, salus.

Nothing remains in one immortal stay,
Bright day is darkened by the shadowy night,
Gay buds are stricken by the sudden cold.
A sadder wind vexes the quiet sea,
And golden youth that once would course the stag
Is stooped above his stick, a tired old man.
O flying world! That we, sick-hearted, love thee!
Still thou escapest, here, there, everywhere,
Slipping down from us. Fly then if thou wilt—
Our hearts are set in the strong love of God.
And may His lovingkindness keep His men
From the dread enemy, and lift their hearts
To Him, our life, our glory, our salvation.

MS. OF MONTE CASSINO

Ad Paulum Diaconum

Hinc celer egrediens facili, mea carta, volatu
per silvas, colles, valles quoque prepete cursu
alma deo cari Benedicti tecta require.
Est nam certa quies fessis venientibus illuc,
hic olus hospitibus, piscis hic, panis abundans;
pax pia, mens humilis, pulcra et concordia fratrum,
laus, amor et cultus Christi simul omnibus horis.

MS. OF MONTE CASSINO

Written to Paul the Deacon at Monte Cassino

Across the hills and through the valley's shade,
  Alone the small script goes,
Seeking for Benedict's beloved roof,
  Where waits its sure repose.
They come and find, the tired travellers,
  Green herbs and ample bread,
Quiet and brothers' love and humbleness,
  Christ's peace on every head.

ANGILBERT

Versus de Bella quae fuit acta Fontaneto

Aurora cum primo mane tetram noctem dividit,
Sabbatum non illud fuit, sed Saturni dolium,
de fraterna rupta pace gaudet demon impius.

Bella clamat, hinc et inde pugna gravis oritur,
frater fratri mortem parat, nepoti avunculus;
filius nec patri suo exhibet quod meruit.

Caedes nulla peior fuit campo nec in Marcio;
fracta est lex christianorum sanguinis proluvio,
unde manus inferorum, gaudet gula Cerberi.

Dextera prepotens dei protexit Hlotharium,
victor ille manu sua pugnavitque fortiter:
ceteri si sic pugnassent, mox foret concordia.

Ecce olim velut Iudas salvatorem tradidit,
sic te, rex, tuique duces tradiderunt gladio;
esto cautus, ne frauderis agnus lupo previo.

Fontaneto fontem dicunt, villam quoque rustici,
ubi strages et ruina Francorum de sanguine;
orrent campi, orrent silvae, orrent ipse paludes.

Gramen illud ros et ymber nec humectat pluvia,
in quo fortes ceciderunt, proelio doctissimi,
pater, mater, soror, frater, quos amici fleverant.

ANGILBERT

On the Battle which was fought at Fontenoy

WHEN the dawn at early morning drove the sullen night away,
Treachery of Saturn was it, not the holy sabbath day.
Over peace of brothers broken joys the Fiend in devilry.

Cry of war is here and yonder, fierce the fighting that
outbroke,
Brother brings to death his brother, this man slays his
sister's son,
Son against his father fighting, ancient kindnesses fordone.

Never was there wilder slaughter, never in the field of Mars,
Law of Christ is broken, broken, Christian blood is shed
like rain,
And the throat of Cerberus belling maketh glad the hosts
of hell.

Strong the hand of God outstretching overshadowed King
Lothair,
Victory came to him fighting with his own arm mightily.
Had all men fought in his fashion, peace had soon returned
there.

Look you, even as once Judas was a traitor to his Lord,
So, O King, thy princes gave thee in betrayal to the sword.
O beware, beware the treason! Lamb, the wolf is in the fold!

Fontenoy they call it, once a springing well and little farm,
There where now is blood and slaughter and the ruin of the
Franks,
Shuddering the fields and copses, shuddering the very
swamp.

On that grass be dew nor shower, nor the freshening of rain,
Where the bravest, battle-wisest bowed themselves and fell
down slain:
Father, mother, sister, brother, friend for friend have wept
in vain.

Hoc autem scelus peractum, quod descripsi ritmice,
Angilbertus, ego vidi pugnansque cum aliis,
solus de multis remansi prima frontis acie.

Ima vallis retrospexi, verticemque iugeri
ubi suos inimicos rex fortis Hlotharius
expugnabat fugientes usque forum rivuli.

Karoli de parte vero, Hludovici pariter
albent campi vestimentis mortuorum lineis,
velut solent in autumno albescere avibus.

Laude pugna non est digna, nec canatur melode,
Oriens, meridianus, Occidens et Aquilo,
plangant illos qui fuerunt illic casu mortui.

Maledicta dies illa, nec in anni circulo
numeretur, sed radatur ab omni memoria,
iubar solis illi desit, aurora crepusculo.

Noxque illa, nox amara, noxque dura nimium,
in qua fortes ceciderunt, proelio doctissimi,
pater, mater, soror, frater, quos amici fleverant.

O luctum atque lamentum! nudati sunt mortui.
horum carnes vultur, corvus, lupus vorant acriter;
orrent, carent sepulturis, vanum iacet cadaver.

Ploratum et ululatum nec describo amplius:
unusquisque quantum potest restringatque lacrimas:
pro illorum animabus deprecemur dominum.

Yea, I Angilbertus saw it, the whole deed of horror done,
I that make a rhyme upon it, there was fighting with the rest,
And alone am left surviving of that foremost battle line.

I looked back upon the valley and the summit of the hill,
When Lothair, strong king and valiant, scattered them
    before his sword,
Drove them flying on before him to the crossing of the ford.

Yea, but whether they were men of Charles or men of
    Louis there,
Now the fields are bleached to whiteness with the white
    shrouds of the slain,
Even as they bleach in autumn with the coming of the gulls.

Be no glory of that battle, never let that fight be sung,
From his rising in the morning to the setting of the sun,
South and North, bewail them who in that ill chance to
    death were done.

Cursed be the day that saw it, in the circuit of the year
Count it not, let it be razèd from the memory of men,
Never shine the sun upon it, nor its twilight break in dawn.

And that night, a night of anguish, night too bitter and too
    hard,
Night that saw them fallen in battle, fallen the wise and
    high of heart:
Father, mother, sister, brother, friend for friend have wept
    in vain.

O the grief and the bewailing! there they lie, the naked dead,
On their bodies wolves and crows and vultures ravin and
    are fed,
There they lie, unburied horror, idle corpses that were men.

On that grief and that bewailing make I now no further
    stay:
To each man his sorrow, let him master it as best he may,
And on all their souls have mercy, God the Lord, let all
    men pray.

HRABANUS MAURUS

Ad Eigilum de libro quem scripserat

Nullum opus exsurgit quod non annosa vetustas
    expugnet, quod non vertat iniqua dies.
grammata sola carent fato, mortemque repellunt.
    preterita renovant grammata sola biblis.
grammata nempe dei digitus sulcabat in apta
    rupe, suo legem cum dederat populo.
sunt, fuerant, mundo venient quae forte futura,
    grammata haec monstrant famine cuncta suo.

HRABANUS MAURUS

To Eigilus, on the book that he had written

No work of men's hands but the weary years
   Besiege and take it, comes its evil day:
The written word alone flouts destiny,
   Revives the past and gives the lie to Death.
God's finger made its furrows in the rock
   In letters, when He gave His folk the law.
And things that are, and have been, and may be,
   Their secret with the written word abides.

HRABANUS MAURUS

Dulcissimo Fratri ac Reverentissimo Abbati Grimoldo

VIVE, meae vires lassarumque anchora rerum,
    naufragio et litus tutaque terra meo,
solus honor nobis, urbs tu fidissima semper
    curisque afflicto tuta quies animo.
sintque licet montes inter cum fluctibus arva
    mens tecum est nulla quae cohibetur humo.
te mea mens sequitur, sequitur quoque carmen amoris,
    exoptans animo prospera cuncta tuo.
qui mihi te notum dedit et concessit amicum
    conservet sanum Christus ubique mihi.
ante solum terrae caelique volubile cyclum
    praetereant, vester quam quoque cesset amor.
hocque, pater, monui, moneo te iterumque monebo,
    sis memor ipse mei, sicut et ipse tui,
ut deus in terris quos hic coniunxit amicos,
    gaudentes pariter iungat in arce poli.

HRABANUS MAURUS

To Grimold, Abbot of St. Gall

THEN live, my strength, anchor of weary ships,
   Safe shore and land at last, thou, for my wreck,
My honour, thou, and my abiding rest,
   My city safe for a bewildered heart.
What though the plains and mountains and the sea
   Between us are, that which no earth can hold
Still follows thee, and love's own singing follows,
   Longing that all things may be well with thee.
Christ who first gave thee for a friend to me,
Christ keep thee well, where'er thou art, for me.
   Earth's self shall go and the swift wheel of heaven
Perish and pass, before our love shall cease.
   Do but remember me, as I do thee,
And God, who brought us on this earth together,
   Bring us together in His house of heaven.

WALAFRID STRABO

Insula Felix

MUSA, nostrum, plange, soror, dolorem,
pande de nostro miserum recessum
heu solo, quem continuo pudenda
    pressit egestas.

Nam miser pectus sapiens habere
quaero, quam ob causam patriam relinquo
et malis tactus variis perosus
    plango colonus . . .

Frigus invadit grave nuditatem,
non calent palmae, pedibus retracta
stat cutis, vultus hiemem pavescit
    valde severam.

In domo frigus patior nivale,
non iuvat cerni gelidum cubile.
nec foris lectove calens repertam
    prendo quietem.

Si tamen nostram veneranda mentem
possidens prudentia contineret
parte vel parva: ingenii calore
    tutior essem.

Heu pater, si solus adesse possis,
quem sequens terrae petii remota,
credo nil laesisse tui misellum
    pectus alumni.

WALAFRID STRABO

Written from Fulda to his old master at Reichenau

SISTER, my Muse, weep thou for me I pray.
Wretched am I that ever went away
From my own land, and am continually
    Ashamed and poor.

Fool that I was, a scholar I would be,
For learning's sake I left my own country,
No luck have I and no man cares for me,
    Exiled and strange.

'Tis bitter frost and I am poorly happed,
I cannot warm my hands, my feet are chapped,
My very face shudders when I go out
    To brave the cold.

Even in the house it is as cold as snow,
My frozen bed's no pleasure to me now,
I'm never warm enough in it to go
    To quiet sleep.

I think perhaps if I had any sense,
Even a little smattering pretence
Of wisdom, I could put up some defence,
    Warmed by my wits.

Alas, my father, if thou wert but here,
At whose behest thy scholar came so far,
I think there is no hurt that could come near
    His foolish heart.

III

Ecce prorumpunt lacrimae, recordor,
quam bona dudum fruerer quiete,
cum daret felix mihimet pusillum
    Augia tectum.

Sancta sis semper nimiumque cara
mater, ex sanctis cuneis dicata,
laude, profectu, meritis, honore,
    insula felix.

Nunc item sanctam liceat vocari
qua dei matris colitur patenter
cultus, ut laeti merito sonemus,
    insula felix.

Tu licet cingaris aquis profundis,
es tamen firmissima caritate,
quae sacra in cunctos documenta spargis,
    insula felix.

Te quidem semper cupiens videre,
per dies noctesque tui recordor,
cuncta quae nobis bona ferre gestis,
    insula felix. . . . .

Donet hoc Christi pietas tonantis,
ut locis gaudere tuis reductus
ordiar, dicens: vale, gloriosa
    mater, in aevum . . .

Da, precor, vitae spatium, redemptor,
donec optatos patriae regressus
in sinus, Christi celebrare laudis
    munera possim.

Now start the sudden tears, remembering
How quiet it was there, the fostering
Of those low roofs that gave me sheltering
  At Reichenau.

O mother of thy sons, beloved, benign,
Thy saints have made thee holy, and the shrine
Of God's own Mother in thy midst doth shine,
  O happy isle.

What though deep waters round about thee are,
Most strong in love stand thy foundations sure,
And holy learning thou hast scattered far,
  O happy isle.

Still cries my heart that blessed place to see,
By day, by night, do I remember thee,
And all the kindness in thy heart for me,
  O happy isle.

Christ in His mercy give to me this grace,
That I may come back to that happy place,
And stand again and bless thee face to face,
  O mother isle.

Let me not die, O Christ, but live so long
To see again the land for which I yearn;
Back to her heart to win at last return,
  And praise Thee there.

WALAFRID STRABO

Commendatio Opusculi De Cultura Hortorum

HAEC tibi servitii munuscula vilia parvi
Strabo tuus, Grimalde pater doctissime, servus
pectore devoto nullius ponderis offert,
ut cum consepto vilis consederis horti
subter opacatas frondenti vertice malos,
persicus imparibus crines ubi dividit umbris,
dum tibi cana legunt tenera lanugine poma
ludentes pueri, scola laetabunda tuorum,
atque volis ingentia mala capacibus indunt,
grandia conantes includere corpora palmis:
quo moneare habeas nostri, pater alme, laboris,
dum relegis quae dedo volens, interque legendum
ut vitiosa seces, deposco, placentia firmes.
te deus aeterna faciat virtute virentem
inmarcescibilis palmam comprendere vitae:
hoc pater, hoc natus, hoc spiritus annuat almus.

WALAFRID STRABO

To Grimold, Abbot of St. Gall, with his book " Of Gardening "

A VERY paltry gift, of no account,
My father, for a scholar like to thee,
But Strabo sends it to thee with his heart.
So might you sit in the small garden close
In the green darkness of the apple trees
Just where the peach tree casts its broken shade,
And they would gather you the shining fruit
With the soft down upon it; all your boys,
Your little laughing boys, your happy school,
And bring huge apples clasped in their two hands.
Something the book may have of use to thee.
Read it, my father, prune it of its faults,
And strengthen with thy praise what pleases thee.
And may God give thee in thy hands the green
Unwithering palm of everlasting life.

WALAFRID STRABO

Ad amicum

Cum splendor lunae fulgescat ab aethere purae,
tu sta sub divo cernens speculamine miro,
qualiter ex luna splendescat lampade pura
et splendore suo caros amplectitur uno
corpore divisos, sed mentis amore ligatos.
si facies faciem spectare nequivit amantem,
hoc saltem nobis lumen sit pignus amoris.
hos tibi versiculos fidus transmisit amicus;
si de parte tua fidei stat fixa catena,
nunc precor, ut valeas felix per saecula cuncta.

WALAFRID STRABO

To his friend in absence

WHEN the moon's splendour shines in naked heaven,
  Stand thou and gaze beneath the open sky.
See how that radiance from her lamp is riven,
  And in one splendour foldeth gloriously
Two that have loved, and now divided far,
Bound by love's bond, in heart together are.

What though thy lover's eyes in vain desire thee,
  Seek for love's face, and find that face denied?
Let that light be between us for a token;
  Take this poor verse that love and faith inscribe.
Love, art thou true? and fast love's chain about thee?
Then for all time, O love, God give thee joy!

SEDULIUS SCOTTUS

Carmen Paschale

SURREXIT Christus sol verus vespere noctis,
    surgit et hinc domini mystica messis agri.
nunc vaga puniceis apium plebs laeta labore
    floribus instrepitans poblite mella legit.
nunc variae volucres permulcent aethera cantu,
    temperat et pernox nunc philomela melos.
nunc chorus ecclesiae cantat per cantica Sion,
    alleluia suis centuplicatque tonis.
Tado, pater patriae, caelestis gaudia paschae
    percipias meritis limina lucis: ave.

SEDULIUS SCOTTUS

Easter Sunday

LAST night did Christ the Sun rise from the dark,
  The mystic harvest of the fields of God,
And now the little wandering tribes of bees
  Are brawling in the scarlet flowers abroad.
The winds are soft with birdsong; all night long
  Darkling the nightingale her descant told,
And now inside church doors the happy folk
  The Alleluia chant a hundredfold.
O father of thy folk, be thine by right
The Easter joy, the threshold of the light.

SEDULIUS SCOTTUS

Ad Hartgarium

NUNC viridant segetes, nunc florent germine campi,
nunc turgent vites, est nunc pulcherrimus annus,
nunc pictae volucres permulcent ethera cantu,
nunc mare, nunc tellus, nunc celi sidera rident.

At non tristificis perturbat potio sucis,
cum medus atque Ceres, cum Bacchi munera desint,
heu—quam multiplicis defit substantia carnis,
quam mitis tellus generat, quam roscidus ether.

Scriptor sum (fateor), sum musicus alter et Orpheus,
sum bos triturans, prospera quaeque volo.
sum vester miles sophie preditus armis;
pro nobis nostrum, Musa, rogato patrem.

SEDULIUS SCOTTUS

He complains to Bishop Hartgar of thirst

THE standing corn is green, the wild in flower,
   The vines are swelling, 'tis the sweet o' the year,
Bright-winged the birds, and heaven shrill with song,
   And laughing sea and earth and every star.

But with it all, there's never a drink for me,
   No wine, nor mead, nor even a drop of beer.
Ah, how hath failed that substance manifold,
   Born of the kind earth and the dewy air!

I am a writer, I, a musician, Orpheus the second,
   And the ox that treads out the corn, and your well-
      wisher I,
I am your champion armed with the weapons of wisdom
    and logic,
   Muse, tell my lord bishop and father his servant is dry.

SEDULIUS SCOTTUS

Apologia pro vita sua

AUT lego vel scribo, doceo scrutorve sophiam:
    obsecro celsithronum nocte dieque meum.
vescor, poto libens, rithmizans invoco Musas,
    dormisco stertens: oro deum vigilans.
conscia mens scelerum deflet peccamina vitae;
    parcite vos misero, Christe Maria, viro.

SEDULIUS SCOTTUS

Written as scholasticus *at Liege*

I READ or write, I teach or wonder what is truth,
    I call upon my God by night and day.
I eat and freely drink, I make my rhymes,
    And snoring sleep, or vigil keep and pray.
And very ware of all my shames I am;
    O Mary, Christ, have mercy on your man.

SEDULIUS SCOTTUS

Contra Plagam

LIBERA plebem tibi servientem,
ira mitescat tua, sancte rector,
lacrimas clemens gemitusque amaros
    respice, Christe.

Tu pater noster dominusque celsus,
nos tui servi sumus, alme pastor,
frontibus nostris rosei cruoris
    signa gerentes.

Infero tristi tibi quis fatetur?
mortui laudes tibi num sacrabunt?
ferreae virgae, metuende iudex,
    parce, rogamus.

Non propinetur populo tuoque
nunc calix irae, meriti furoris:
clareant priscae miserationes—
    quaesumus, audi.

Deleas nostrum facinus, precamur,
nosque conserva, benedicte princeps,
mentium furvas supera tenebras,
    lux pia mundi.

Sancte sanctorum, dominusque regum,
visitet plebem tua sancta dextra,
nos tuo vultu videas serenus,
    ne pereamus.

SEDULIUS SCOTTUS

Intercession against the Plague

Set free Thy people, set free Thy servants,
Lighten Thine anger, Ruler most holy;
Look on their anguish, bitter their weeping,
    Christ, in Thy mercy.

Thou art our Father, Master exalted,
We are Thy servants, Thou the Good Shepherd,
Bearing Thy token of blood and of crimson
    Marked on our foreheads.

Deep in Thy hell who then shall confess Thee?
Yea, shall the dead give praise to Thy name?
Judge of our dread, Thy rod is of iron,
    Spare us, we pray Thee.

Bring not so near to Thy people, Thy servants,
The cup of Thine anger, Thy merited wrath:
Lighten upon us Thine ancient compassion.
    We cry. Do Thou hear!

Loosen, we pray Thee, our load of transgression.
Vouchsafe to keep us, Prince ever blessed.
Vanquish the shadow that darkens our spirits,
    Light of the world.

Saint of all saints and king of all kingships,
Visit Thy people with Thy right hand.
Lift up the light of Thy countenance upon us,
    Lord, or we perish.

NINTH CENTURY MS. OF VERONA

Andecavis Abbas

ANDECAVIS	abas esse dicitur
ille nomen	primi tenet hominum;
hunc fatentur	vinum vellet bibere
super omnes	Andechavis homines.

Eia eia eia laudes
Eia laudes dicamus Libero.

Iste malet	vinum omne tempore
quem nec dies	nox nec ulla preterit
quod non vino	saturatus titubet,
velut arbor	agitata flatibus.

Eia eia eia laudes
Eia laudes dicamus Libero.

Iste gerit	corpus imputribile
vinum totum	conditum ut alove
et ut mire	corium conficitur
cutis eius	nunc cum vino tingitur.

Eia eia eia laudes
Eia lauda dicamus Libero.

Iste cupa	non curat de calicem
vinum bonum	bibere suaviter,
sed patellis	atque magnis cacabis
et in eis	ultra modum grandibus.

Eia eia eia laudes
Eia laudes dicamus Libero.

NINTH CENTURY MS. OF VERONA

The Abbot Adam of Angers

ONCE there was an   Abbot of Angers.
And the name of   the first man did he bear.
And they say he   had a mighty thirst
Even beyond the   townsmen of Angers.
Ho and ho and ho and ho !
Glory be to Bacchus !

He would have his   wine all times and seasons
Never did a   day or night go by,
But it found him   wine-soaked and wavering
Even as a tree   that the high winds sway
Ho and ho and ho and ho !
Glory be to Bacchus !

As to body   was he incorruptible.
Like a wine that's   spiced with bitter aloes.
And as hides are   dressed and tanned with myrrh,
So was his skin   deep-tanned with wine.
Ho and ho and ho and ho !
Glory be to Bacchus !

Nor did he like   elegantly drinking
From a wine cup   filled from the barrel.
Naught would do him but mighty pots and pannikins,
Pots and pans still   greater than their species.
Ho and ho and ho and ho !
Glory be to Bacchus !

Hunc perperdet   Andechavis civitas,
nullum talem   ultra sibi sociat,
qui sic semper   vinum possit sorbere;
cuius facta,   cives, vobis pingite!
Eia eia eia laudes
Eia laudes dicamus Libero.

Should it hap that   the town of Angers lost him,
Never would it   see his like again
Never see his   like for steady drinking.
Mark him well, ye   townsmen of Angers.
Ho and ho and ho and ho !
Glory be to Bacchus !

RADBOD

" Anno ab incarnatione domini DCCCC apparuit in caelo mirabile signum. stelle enim vise sunt undique tamen ex alto in orizontis ima profluere, circa poli cardinem omnes fere inter se concurrere. quod prodigium secute sunt tristes rerum kalamitates : aeris videlicet maxima intemperies crebrique ventorum turbines, fluminum quoque terminos suos transgredientium terribilis quedam quasi Kataclismi imago et (quod his pestilentius est) dire hominum adversus deum se extollentium tempestates. hoc eodem anno, priusquam epacte mutarentur, Folko Remorum metropolitanus et Zvendiboldus rex interfecti sunt, ac non multis antea diebus ego peccator Radbodus inter famulos sancte Traiectensis ecclesie conscribi merui ; atque o utinam cum eisdem eterne vite consortium merear adipisci. hoc ergo erit epitaphium meum :

> aesuries te, Christe deus, sitis atque videndi
> iam modo carnales me vetat esse dapes.
> da modo te vesci, te potum haurire salutis ;
> unicus ignote tu cybus esto vie.
> et quem longa fames errantem ambesit in orbe,
> nunc satia vultu, patris imago, tuo.''

RADBOD

" In the year of the Incarnation of our Lord 900 there appeared a marvellous sign in heaven. For the stars were seen to flow from the very height of heaven to the lowest horizon, wellnigh as though they crashed one upon the other. And upon this marvel followed woeful calamities, such as a most notable untowardness of the seasons and frequent tempests, rivers also overflowing their banks as in dread likeness of the Deluge and (what was yet more pestilent than these) ominous upheavals of men boasting themselves against God. In this same year, ere the intercalary days were ended, Fulk the archbishop of Rheims and the king Zvendibold were slain, and not many days before, I, Radbod the sinner, was judged worthy to be enrolled among the servants of the holy church of Utrecht: and O would that I be found worthy of that same company in the life eternal. This then shall be my epitaph:

> Hunger and thirst, O Christ, for sight of Thee,
> Came between me and all the feasts of earth.
> Give Thou Thyself the Bread, Thyself the Wine,
> Thou, sole provision for the unknown way.
> Long hunger wasted the world wanderer,
> With sight of Thee may he be satisfied."

RADBOD

De Hirundine

FLORIFERAS auras et frondea tempora capto
   tumque per humanas hospitor ipsa domos
atque ibi spectandum cunctis confingo cubile,
   segnis inersque manus quale patrare nequit.
in quo nata mihi praedulcia pignora servo
   donec me valeant per spatia ampla sequi.
hunc mihi iungo gregem, et volucres mox explico pennas,
   impigra sic totam duco volando diem.
nec tamen id frustra; dum quippe per ardua trano,
   arrident densis aethera laeta satis.
at, cum limosas pennis contingo paludes,
   tum pluvia et ventis, Æole, tundis agros.

RADBOD

The Swallow

I TAKE the winds flower-bringing,
  I take the time of leaves,
And tarry in men's houses,
  Building beneath the eaves

My nest where all can see it;
  And there I keep my young,
My brood so sweet and little,
  Until their time is come.

Out in the empty spaces
  They follow me away,
Swift are my wings and tireless
  All the long summer day.

And up in those high places
  My flight is not in vain,
For kindly laughs the joyous sun
  On fields of standing grain.

But when in the dank marshes
  I dip a flying wing,
Then through the fields comes flailing
  The east wind harsh with rain.

sole dehinc gelido cum ninguida bruma propinquat
  seu patria pellor seu fugio ipsa mea.
nec dulces nidos nec hospita limina curans,
  sed propriae sortis indita iura sequens.
sic rigidas auras ignotis vito sub antris,
  sic quoque naturae do paradigma tenax.
heus homo, dum causas rerum miraris opertas,
  ne spernas decoris munera quaeso tui.
tu ratione viges—ego sum rationis egena:
  tu post fata manes—fata ego tota sequor.
his quantum superas, tantum me vince creantis
  imperio parens, iussit ut ipse creans.

Colder the sun, and winter,
  Bitter with snow at hand.
Out-driven or out-flying,
  I leave my fatherland.

Sweet nests and kindly threshold,
  Unheeding leave behind,
And my own fate I follow,
  Far from the frozen wind.

Beneath strange roofs I shelter.
  O man, wilt thou not see?
I follow fate: why wilt thou
  Lag after destiny?

EUGENIUS VULGARIUS

Metrum Parhemiacum Tragicum

O TRISTIA secla priora,
que vos docuere sepulcra
animisque parando nociva
belli fabricare pericla?

Heu quis prior ille piator
qui cusor in arte fabrina
variavit in igne figuras,
cudens gladii male formas?

Quis denique Martia primus
arcus volucresque sagittas
ignivit et edidit iras,
mortes stabilivit amaras?

Qui spicula cudit in usus,
conflavit in incude funus;
lamne tenuavit et ictus,
ventris vacuaret ut haustus.

Docuit quoque cuspide mortem
qui duxit in ordine martem;
amiserat et quia mentem
umbre tenuere tumentem.

EUGENIUS VULGARIUS

Written c. 900

O sorrowful and ancient days,
  Where learned ye to make sepulchres?
Who taught you all the evil ways
  Wherein to wound men's souls in wars?

Woe to that sacrificial priest,
  First craftsman of the blacksmith's forge,
Who saw strange shapes within his fire,
  And hammered out illgotten swords.

Whoever fashioned first the bow,
  And flight of arrows, swift, secure,
Launched anger on the air and made
  The bitterness of death more sure.

Who tempered spearheads for their work,
  He breathed upon the anvil death;
He hammered out the slender blade,
  And from the body crushed the breath.

He gave to death a thrusting spear,
  Who first drew up his battle-hosts.
Long since hath fared his vaunting soul
  To dwell a ghost amid the ghosts.

TENTH CENTURY MS.

Alba

Phoebi claro nondum orto iubare,
fert Aurora   lumen terris tenue:
spiculator   pigris clamat ' surgite.'
L'alba part umet mar atra sol
Poy pasa bigil mira clar tenebras.

En incautos   hostium insidie
torpentesque gliscunt intercipere
quos suadet   preco clamans surgere.
L'alba part umet mar atra sol
Poy pasa bigil mira clar tenebras.

Ab Arcturo   disgregatur aquilo
poli suos   condunt astra radios.
orienti   tenditur septentrio.
L'alba part umet mar atra sol
Poy pasa bigil mira clar tenebras.

TENTH CENTURY MS.

Aubade

HYPERION's clear star is not yet risen,
Dawn brings a tenuous light across the earth,
The watcher to the sleeper cries, " Arise! "
  Dawn over the dark sea brings on the sun ;
  She leans across the hilltop : see, the light !

Behold the ambush of the enemy
Stealing to take the heedless in their sleep,
And still the herald's voice that cries " Arise! "
  Dawn over the dark sea brings on the sun ;
  She leans across the hilltop : see, the light !

The North wind from Arcturus now blows free,
The stars go into hiding in the sky,
And nearer to the sunrise swings the Plough.
  Dawn over the dark sea brings on the sun ;
  She leans across the hilltop : see, the light !

MS. OF ST. MARTIAL OF LIMOGES

De Sancto Michaele

PLEBS angelica,
phalanx et archangelica
principans turma, virtus
Uranica,
ac potestas
almiphona.

Dominantia
numina divinaque
subsellia, Cherubim
aetherea
ac Seraphim
ignicoma,

Vos, O Michael
caeli satrapa,
Gabrielque vera
dans verba nuntia,

Atque Raphael,
vitae vernula,
transferte nos inter
Paradisicolas.

MS. OF ST. MARTIAL OF LIMOGES

For St. Michael

Angelic host,
Phalanx and squadron of the Prince-Archangels,
Uranian power,
Strength of the gracious word,

Spirits that have dominion, Cherubim,
Divine tribunal of the air,
And Seraphim with flaming hair,

And you, O Michael, Prince of heaven,
And Gabriel, by whom the word was given,

And Raphael, born in the house of Life,
Bring us among the folk of Paradise.

VESTIUNT SILVE

Vestiunt silve tenera merorem
virgulta, suis onerata pomis,
canunt de celsis sedibus palumbes
carmina cunctis.

Hic turtur gemit, resonat hic turdus,
pangit hic priscus merularum sonus;
passer nec tacens, arridens garritu
alte sub ulmis.

Hic leta canit philomela frondis
longas effundit sibilum per auras
sollempne, milvus tremulaque voce
aethera pulsat.

Ad astra volans aquila, in auris
alauda canit, modulis resoluit,
desursum vergit dissimili modo,
dum terram tangit.

Velox impulit rugitus hirundo,
clangit coturnix, gracula fringultit;
aves sic cuncte celebrant estivum
undique carmen.

Nulla inter aves similis est api,
que talem gerit tipum castitatis
nisi Maria, que Christum portavit alvo
inviolata.

MSS. OF CANTERBURY AND VERONA

THE sadness of the wood is bright
With young green sprays, the apple trees
Are laden, in their nests high overhead
      Wood pigeons croon.

The doves make moan, deep throated sings the thrush,
The blackbirds flute their ancient melody;
The sparrow twitters, making his small jests
      High underneath the elm.

The nightingale sings happy in the leaves,
Pouring out on the winds far carrying
Her solemn melody: the sudden hawk
      Quavers in the high air.

The eagle takes his flight against the sun;
High overhead the lark trills in the sky,
Down dropping from her height and changing note,
      She touches earth.

Swift darting swallows utter their low cry;
The jackdaw jargons, and clear cries the quail;
And so in every spot some bird is singing
      A summer song.

Yet none among the birds is like the bee,
Who is the very type of chastity,
Save she who bore the burden that was Christ
      In her inviolate womb.

IAM, DULCIS AMICA

Tenth Century

Iam, dulcis amica, venito,
quam sicut cor meum diligo;
Intra in cubiculum meum,
ornamentis cunctis onustum.

Ibi sunt sedilia strata
et domus velis ornata,
Floresque in domo sparguntur
herbeque fragrantes miscentur.

Est ibi mensa apposita
universis cibis onusta:
Ibi clarum vinum abundat
et quidquid te, cara, delectat.

Ibi sonant dulces symphonie
inflantur et altius tibie;
Ibi puer et docta puella
pangunt tibi carmina bella:

Hic cum plectro citharam tangit,
illa melos cum lira pangit;
Portantque ministri pateras
pigmentatis poculis plenas.

MSS. OF SALZBURG, CANTERBURY AND LIMOGES

Come, sweetheart, come,
　　Dear as my heart to me,
Come to the room
　　I have made fine for thee.

Here there be couches spread,
　　Tapestry tented,
Flowers for thee to tread,
　　Green herbs sweet scented.

Here is the table spread,
　　Love, to invite thee,
Clear is the wine and red,
　　Love, to delight thee.

Sweet sounds the viol,
　　Shriller the flute,
A lad and a maiden
　　Sing to the lute.

He'll touch the harp for thee,
　　She'll sing the air,
They will bring wine for thee,
　　Choice wine and rare.

Non me iuvat tantum convivium
quantum post dulce colloquium,
Nec rerum tantarum ubertas
ut dilecta familiaritas.

Iam nunc veni, soror electa
et pre cunctis mihi dilecta,
Lux mee clara pupille
parsque maior anime mee.

Ego fui sola in silva
et dilexi loca secreta:
Frequenter effugi tumultum
et vitavi populum multum.

Iam nix glaciesque liquescit,
Folium et herba virescit,
Philomena iam cantat in alto,
Ardet amor cordis in antro.

Karissima, noli tardare;
studeamus nos nunc amare,
Sine te non potero vivere;
iam decet amorem perficere.

Quid iuvat deferre, electa,
que sunt tamen post facienda?
Fac cita quod eris factura,
in me non est aliqua mora.

Yet for this care not I,
   'Tis what comes after,
Not all this lavishness,
   But thy dear laughter.

Mistress mine, come to me,
   Dearest of all,
Light of mine eyes to me,
   Half of my soul.

Alone in the wood
   I have loved hidden places,
Fled from the tumult,
   And crowding of faces.

Now the snow's melting,
   Out the leaves start,
The nightingale's singing,
   Love's in the heart.

Dearest, delay not,
   Ours love to learn,
I live not without thee,
   Love's hour is come.

What boots delay, Love,
   Since love must be?
Make no more stay, Love,
   I wait for thee.

HERIGER

HERIGER, urbis
Maguntiensis
antistes, quendam
vidit prophetam
qui ad infernum
se dixit raptum.

Inde cum multas
referret causas,
subiunxit totum
esse infernum
accinctum densis
undique silvis.

Heriger illi
ridens respondit;
" meum subulcum
illuc ad pastum
volo cum macris
mittere porcis."

HERIGER, BISHOP OF MAINZ

HERIGER,
Bishop of
Mainz, saw a
Prophet who
Said he had
Been carried
Off down to
Hell.

He among
Other and
Divers things
Mentioned that
Hell is sur-
rounded by
Very thick
Woods.

Then the good
Bishop made
Smilingly
Answer: " I
Think I shall
Send to that
Pasture my
Swineherd and
Bid him take
With him my
Very lean
Pigs."

Vir ait falsus:
" fui translatus
in templum celi
Christumque vidi
letum sedentem
et comedentem.

Ioannes baptista
erat pincerna
atque preclari
pocula vini
porrexit cunctis
vocatis sanctis."

.   .   .   .   .   .

Heriger ait:
" prudenter egit
Christus Iohannem
ponens pincernam,
quoniam vinum
non bibit unquam.

The liar said:
" I was to
Heaven trans-
-lated and
Saw Christ there
Sitting and
Joyfully
Eating.

" John called the
Baptist was
Cupbearer,
Handing round
Goblets of
Excellent
Wine to the
Saints."

.   .   .   .   .

The Bishop
Said, " Wisely
Did Christ choose
The Baptist
To be his
Cupbearer,
Because he
Is known not
To drink any
Wine.

Mendax probaris
cum Petrum dicis
illic magistrum
esse cocorum.
est quia summi
ianitor celi.

Honore quali
te deus celi
habuit ibi?
ubi sedisti?
volo ut narres
quid manducasses."

Respondit homo:
" angulo uno
partem pulmonis
furabar cocis:
hoc manducavi
atque recessi."

" But you are
A liar to
Say that St.
Peter is
Head of the
Cooks, when he
Keeps Heaven's
Gate.

" But tell me,
What honour
Did God set
Upon you?
Where did you
Sit?   And on
What did you
Sup? "

He answered:
" I sat in
A corner
And munched at
A piece of a
Lung that I
Stole from the
Cooks."

Heriger illum
iussit ad palum
loris ligari
scopisque cedi,
sermone duro
hunc arguendo:

" Si te ad suum
invitet pastum
Christus, ut secum
capias cibum
cave ne furtum
facias [spurcum].

Heriger
Had him trussed
Up to a
Pillar and
Beaten with
Broom-sticks, the
While he ad-
-dressed him with
Words that were
Harsh.

" If Christ to
His Table
Hereafter
Invites you,
Do not be
In future
So dirty a
Thief."

LEVIS EXSURGIT ZEPHYRUS

Levis exsurgit Zephyrus,
et sol procedit tepidus;
iam terra sinus aperit,
dulcore suo diffluit.

Ver purpuratum exiit,
ornatus suos induit:
aspergit terram floribus,
ligna silvarum frondibus.

Struunt lustra quadrupedes,
et dulces nidos volucres;
inter ligna florentia
sua decantant gaudia.

Quod oculis dum video
et auribus dum audio,
heu, pro tantis gaudiis
tantis inflor suspiriis.

Cum mihi sola sedeo
et hec revolvens palleo,
si forte caput sublevo,
nec audio nec video.

Tu saltim, Veris gratia,
exaudi et considera
frondes, flores et gramina;
nam mea languet anima.

MS. OF ST. AUGUSTINE AT CANTERBURY

SOFTLY the west wind blows;
Gaily the warm sun goes;
The earth her bosom sheweth,
And with all sweetness floweth.

Goes forth the scarlet spring,
Clad with all blossoming,
Sprinkles the fields with flowers,
Leaves on the forest

Dens for four-footed things,
Sweet nests for all with wings.
On every blossomed bough
Joy ringeth now.

I see it with my eyes,
I hear it with my ears,
But in my heart are sighs,
And I am full of tears.

Alone with thought I sit,
And blench, remembering it;
Sometimes I lift my head,
I neither hear nor see.

Do thou, O Spring most fair,
Squander thy care
On flower and leaf and grain.
—Leave me alone with pain!

157

SIGEBERT OF GEMBLOUX

Virginalis sancta frequentia

HINC virginalis sancta frequentia,
Gertrudis, Agnes, Prisca, Cecilia,
   Lucia, Petronilla, Tecla,
    Agatha, Barbara, Juliana,

Multeque quarum nomina non lego,
aut lecta nunc his addere negligo,
   dignas Deo quas fecit esse
    integritas anime fidesque . . .

He pervagantes prata recentia
pro velle querunt serta decentia,
   rosas legentes passionis
    lilia vel violas amoris.

SIGEBERT OF GEMBLOUX

The Virgin Martyrs

THEREFORE come they, the crowding maidens,
Gertrude, Agnes, Prisca, Cecily,
Lucy, Thekla, Juliana,
Barbara, Agatha, Petronel.

And other maids whose names I have read not,
Names I have read and now record not,
But their soul and their faith were maimed not,
  Worthy now of God's company.

Wandering through the fresh fields go they,
Gathering flowers to make them a nosegay,
Gathering roses red for the Passion,
  Lilies and violets for love.

SIGEBERT OF GEMBLOUX

Passio Sanctorum Thebeorum

Conatus roseas Thebeis ferre coronas . . .
lilia nulla mihi, violę nullę, rosa nulla,
lilia munditię rosa carnis mortificandę,
nec per pallorem violę testantur amorem
quo pia sponsa calet, quo sponsus mutuo languet . . .
nescio luteola vaccinia pingere caltha,
non cum narcisso mihi summa papavera carpo,
hic flores desunt inscripti nomina regum.

Quod solum potui studio ludente socordi
alba ligustra mihi iam sponte cadentia legi,
pollice nec pueri dignata nec ungue puellę,
inde rudi textu, non coniuncto bene textu
conserui parvas has qualescunque coronas.
vos, O Thebei, gratissima nomina regi,
votis posco piis, hęc serta locare velitis
inter victrices lauros ederasque virentes.
si rude vilet opus, si rerum futile pondus,
at non vilescat, pia quod devotio praestat.

SIGEBERT OF GEMBLOUX

The Martyrdom of the Theban Legion

I TRIED to make a garland for the saints. . . .
No lily for me, violet or rose,
Lilies for purity, roses for passion denied,
Nor violets wan, to show with what pure fire
The bride for the bridegroom burns.
I cannot gild my berries marigold.
Proud poppies and narcissus not for me,
Nor flowers written with the names of kings.
All that this blockhead zeal of mine could find
Was privet blossom, falling as I touched it,
That never boy or girl would stoop to gather,
And of it, badly woven, ill contrived,
I twisted these poor crowns.
Will you but deign to wear them,
Hide neath the victor's laurel this poor wreath—
Clumsy the work, a silly weight to carry,
And yet revile it not, for it is love.

PETER ABELARD

Sabbato ad Vesperas

O QUANTA qualia
  sunt illa sabbata,
quae semper celebrat
  superna curia,
quae fessis requies,
  quae merces fortibus,
cum erit omnia
  deus in omnibus.

Vera Jerusalem
  est illa civitas
cuius pax iugis est,
  summa iucunditas:
ubi non praevenit
  rem desiderium,
nec desiderio
  minus est praemium.

Quis Rex, quae curia,
  quale palatium,
quae pax, quae requies,
  quod illud gaudium,
huius participes
  exponant gloriae,
si quantum sentiunt
  possint exprimere.

PETER ABELARD

Vespers : Saturday evening

How mighty are the Sabbaths,
  How mighty and how deep,
That the high courts of heaven
  To everlasting keep.
What peace unto the weary,
  What pride unto the strong,
When God in Whom are all things
  Shall be all things to men.

Jerusalem is the city
  Of everlasting peace,
A peace that is surpassing
  And utter blessedness;
Where finds the dreamer waking
  Truth beyond dreaming far,
Nor there the heart's possessing
  Less than the heart's desire.

But of the courts of heaven
  And Him who is the King,
The rest and the refreshing,
  The joy that is therein,
Let those that know it answer
  Who in that bliss have part,
If any word can utter
  The fullness of the heart.

Nostrum est interim
  mentem erigere
et totis patriam
  votis appetere,
et ad Jerusalem
  a Babylonia
post longa regredi
  tandem exsilia.

Illic, molestiis
  finitis omnibus,
securi cantica
  Sion cantabimus,
et iuges gratias
  de donis gratiae
beata referet
  plebs tibi, Domine.

Illic ex Sabbato
  succedit Sabbatum,
perpes laetitia
  sabbatizantium,
nec ineffabilis
  cessabunt iubili,
quos decantabimus
  et nos et angeli.

Perenni Domino
  perpes sit gloria,
ex quo sunt, per quem sunt,
  in quo sunt omnia.
ex quo sunt, Pater est,
  per quem sunt, Filius,
in quo sunt, Patris et
  filii Spiritus.

But ours, with minds uplifted
  Unto the heights of God,
With our whole heart's desiring,
  To take the homeward road,
And the long exile over,
  Captive in Babylon,
Again unto Jerusalem,
  To win at last return.

There, all vexation ended,
  And from all grieving free,
We sing the song of Zion
  In deep security.
And everlasting praises
  For all Thy gifts of grace
Rise from Thy happy people,
  Lord of our blessedness.

There Sabbath unto Sabbath
  Succeeds eternally,
The joy that has no ending
  Of souls in holiday.
And never shall the rapture
  Beyond all mortal ken
Depart the eternal chorus
  That angels sing with men.

Now to the King Eternal
  Be praise eternally,
From whom are all things, by whom
  And in whom all things be.
From Whom, as from the Father,
  By Whom, as by the Son,
In Whom, as in the Spirit,
  God the Lord, Three in One.

PETER ABELARD

In Parasceve Domini : III. Nocturno

Solus ad victimam procedis, Domine,
morti te offerens quam venis tollere:
quid nos miserrimi possumus dicere
qui quae commisimus scimus te luere?

Nostra sunt, Domine, nostra sunt crimina:
quid tua criminum facis supplicia?
quibus sic compati fac nostra pectora,
ut vel compassio digna sit venia.

Nox ista flebilis praesensque triduum
quod demorabitur fletus sit vesperum,
donec laetitiae mane gratissimum
surgente Domino sit maestis redditum.

Tu tibi compati sic fac nos, Domine,
tuae participes ut simus gloriae;
sic praesens triduum in luctu ducere,
ut risum tribuas paschalis gratiae.

PETER ABELARD

Good Friday : the Third Nocturn

ALONE to sacrifice Thou goest, Lord,
Giving Thyself to death whom Thou wilt slay.
For us Thy wretched folk is any word,
Whose sins have brought Thee to this agony ?

For they are ours, O Lord, our deeds, our deeds.
Why must Thou suffer torture for our sin ?
Let our hearts suffer for Thy passion, Lord,
That very suffering may Thy mercy win.

This is that night of tears, the three days' space,
    Sorrow abiding of the eventide,
Until the day break with the risen Christ,
    And hearts that sorrowed shall be satisfied.

So may our hearts share in Thine anguish, Lord,
    That they may sharers of Thy glory be :
Heavy with weeping may the three days pass,
    To win the laughter of Thine Easter Day.

PETER ABELARD

Planctus

VEL confossus pariter
morerer feliciter
cum, quid amor faciat,
maius hoc non habeat,
et me post te vivere
mori sit assidue,
nec ad vitam anima
satis sit dimidia.

Vicem amicitiae
vel unam me reddere
oportebat tempore
summae tunc angustiae,
triumphi participem
vel ruinae comitem,
ut te vel eriperem
vel tecum occumberem,
vitam pro te finiens
quam salvasti totiens,
ut et mors nos iungeret
magis quam disiungeret. . . .

Do quietem fidibus:
vellem, ut et planctibus
sic possem et fletibus:
laesis pulsu manibus
raucis planctu vocibus
deficit et spiritus.

PETER ABELARD

David's Lament for Jonathan

Low in thy grave with thee
　　Happy to lie,
Since there's no greater thing left Love to do;
　　And to live after thee
　　　　Is but to die,
　　For with but half a soul what can Life do?

　　So share thy victory,
　　　　Or else thy grave,
　Either to rescue thee, or with thee lie:
　　Ending that life for thee,
　　　　That thou didst save,
　So Death that sundereth might bring more nigh.

　　Peace, O my stricken lute!
　　　Thy strings are sleeping.
　Would that my heart could still
　　　Its bitter weeping!

THE ARCHPOET

Confessio

Estuans intrinsecus
ira vehementi
in amaritudine
loquar meę menti:
factus de materia
levis elementi
similis sum folio
de quo ludent venti.

Cum sit enim proprium
viro sapienti
supra petram ponere
sedem fundamenti,
stultus ego comparor
fluvio labenti,
sub eodem aere
nunquam permanenti.

Feror ego veluti
sine nauta navis,
ut per vias aeris
vaga fertur avis,
non me tenent vincula,
non me tenet clavis,
quęro mihi similes,
et adiungor pravis.

THE ARCHPOET

His Confession

SEETHING over inwardly
　　With fierce indignation,
In my bitterness of soul,
　　Hear my declaration.
I am of one element,
　　Levity my matter,
Like enough a withered leaf
　　For the winds to scatter.

Since it is the property
　　Of the sapient
To sit firm upon a rock,
　　It is evident
That I am a fool, since I
　　Am a flowing river,
Never under the same sky,
　　Transient for ever.

Hither, thither, masterless
　　Ship upon the sea,
Wandering through the ways of air,
　　Go the birds like me.
Bound am I by ne'er a bond,
　　Prisoner to no key,
Questing go I for my kind,
　　Find depravity.

Mihi cordis gravitas
res videtur gravis;
iocus est amabilis
dulciorque favis;
quicquid Venus imperat
labor est suavis,
quę numquam in cordibus
habitat ignavis.

Via lata gradior
more iuventutis,
implico me vitiis
inmemor virtutis,
voluptatis avidus
magis quam salutis,
mortuus in anima
curam gero cutis.

Pręsul discretissime,
veniam te precor:
morte bona morior,
dulci nece necor,
meum pectus sauciat
puellarum decor,
et quas tactu nequeo,
saltem corde męchor.

Never yet could I endure
  Soberness and sadness,
Jests I love and sweeter than
  Honey find I gladness.
Whatsoever Venus bids
  Is a joy excelling,
Never in an evil heart
  Did she make her dwelling.

Down the broad way do I go,
  Young and unregretting,
Wrap me in my vices up,
  Virtue all forgetting,
Greedier for all delight
  Than heaven to enter in:
Since the soul in me is dead,
  Better save the skin.

Pardon, pray you, good my lord,
  Master of discretion,
But this death I die is sweet,
  Most delicious poison.
Wounded to the quick am I
  By a young girl's beauty:
She's beyond my touching? Well,
  Can't the mind do duty?

Res est arduissima
vincere naturam,
in aspectu virginis
mentem esse puram;
iuvenes non possumus
legem sequi duram,
leviumque corporum
non habere curam.

Quis in igne positus
igne non uratur?
Quis Papię demorans
castus habeatur,
ubi Venus digito
iuvenes venatur,
oculis illaqueat,
facie pręedatur?

Si ponas Ypolitum
hodie Papie,
non erit Ypolitus
in sequenti die:
Veneris in thalamos
ducunt omnes vie,
non est in tot turribus
turris Aricie.

Hard beyond all hardness, this
   Mastering of Nature:
Who shall say his heart is clean,
   Near so fair a creature?
Young are we, so hard a law,
   How should we obey it?
And our bodies, they are young,
   Shall they have no say in't?

Sit you down amid the fire,
   Will the fire not burn you?
To Pavia come, will you
   Just as chaste return you?
Pavia, where Beauty draws
   Youth with finger-tips,
Youth entangled in her eyes,
   Ravished with her lips.

Let you bring Hippolytus,
   In Pavia dine him,
Never more Hippolytus
   Will the morning find him.
In Pavia not a road
   But leads to venery,
Nor among its crowding towers
   One to chastity.

Secundo redarguor
etiam de ludo.
Sed cum ludus corpore
me dimittat nudo,
frigidus exterius
mentis estu sudo,
tunc versus et carmina
meliora cudo.

Tertio capitulo
memoro tabernam.
Illam nullo tempore
sprevi, neque spernam,
donec sanctos angelos
venientes cernam,
cantantes pro mortuis
" Requiem eternam."

Meum est propositum
in taberna mori,
ut sint vina proxima
morientis ori;
tunc cantabunt letius
angelorum chori:
" Deus sit propitius
huic potatori."

Yet a second charge they bring:
   I'm for ever gaming.
Yea, the dice hath many a time
   Stripped me to my shaming.
What an if the body's cold,
   If the mind is burning,
On the anvil hammering,
   Rhymes and verses turning?

Look again upon your list.
   Is the tavern on it?
Yea, and never have I scorned,
   Never shall I scorn it,
Till the holy angels come,
   And my eyes discern them,
Singing for the dying soul,
   Requiem aeternam.

For on this my heart is set:
   When the hour is nigh me,
Let me in the tavern die,
   With a tankard by me,
While the angels looking down
   Joyously sing o'er me,
Deus sit propitius
   Huic potatori.

Poculis accenditur
animi lucerna,
cor inbutum nectare
volat ad superna;
mihi sapit dulcius
vinum de taberna,
quam quod aqua miscuit
presulis pincerna.

Loca vitant publica
quidam poetarum,
et secretas eligunt
sedes latebrarum,
student, instant, vigilant,
nec laborant parum,
et vix tandem reddere
possunt opus clarum.

Ieiunant et abstinent
poetarum chori,
vitant rixas publicas
et tumultus fori,
et, ut opus faciant
quod non possit mori,
moriuntur studio
subditi labori.

'Tis the fire that's in the cup
   Kindles the soul's torches,
'Tis the heart that drenched in wine
   Flies to heaven's porches.
Sweeter tastes the wine to me
   In a tavern tankard
Than the watered stuff my Lord
   Bishop hath decanted.

Let them fast and water drink,
   All the poets' chorus,
Fly the market and the crowd
   Racketing uproarious :
Sit in quiet spots and think,
   Shun the tavern's portal,
Write, and never having lived,
   Die to be immortal.

Mihi nunquam spiritus
poetrie datur,
nisi prius fuerit
venter bene satur;
dum in arce cerebri
Bachus dominatur,
in me Phebus irruit,
et miranda fatur.

Unicuique proprium
dat natura munus,
ego numquam potui
scribere ieiunus.
me ieiunum vincere
posset puer unus,
sitem et ieiunium
odi tamquam funus.

Unicuique proprium
dat natura donum;
ego versus faciens
bibo vinum bonum,
et quod habent purius
dolia cauponum,
tale vinum generat
copiam sermonum. . . . .

Never hath the spirit of
   Poetry descended,
Till with food and drink my lean
   Belly was distended,
But when Bacchus lords it in
   My cerebral story,
Comes Apollo with a rush,
   Fills me with his glory.

Unto every man his gift.
   Mine was not for fasting.
Never could I find a rhyme
   With my stomach wasting.
As the wine is, so the verse:
   'Tis a better chorus
When the landlord hath a good
   Vintage set before us.

Ecce, meę proditor
pravitatis fui,
de qua me redarguunt
servientes tui.
sed eorum nullus est
accusator sui,
quamvis velint ludere
seculoque frui.

Iam nunc in praesentia
presulis beati,
secundum dominici
regulam mandati
mittat in me lapidem,
neque parcat vati
cuius non sit animus
conscius peccati. . . . .

Good my lord, the case is heard,
  I myself betray me,
And affirm myself to be
  All my fellows say me.
See, they in thy presence are :
  Let whoe'er hath known
His own heart and found it clean,
  Cast at me the stone.

MS. OF BENEDICTBEUERN

POTATORES exquisiti,
licet sitis sine siti,
et bibatis expediti
et scyphorum inobliti,
scyphi crebro repetiti
    non dormiant,
et sermones inauditi
    prosiliant.

Qui potare non potestis,
    ite procul ab his festis,
non est locus hic modestis.
Inter letos mos agrestis
    modestie,
et est sue certus testis
    ignavie.

Si quis latitat hic forte,
qui non curat vinum forte,
ostendantur illi porte,
exeat ab hac cohorte:
plus est nobis gravis morte,
    si maneat,
si recedat a consorte,
    tunc pereat.

MS. OF BENEDICTBEUERN

To you, consummate drinkers,
　Though little be your drought,
Good speed be to your tankards,
　And send the wine about.
Let not the full decanter
　Sleep on its round,
And may unheard of banter
　In wit abound.

If any cannot carry
　His liquor as he should,
Let him no longer tarry,
　No place here for the prude.
No room among the happy
　For modesty.
A fashion only fit for clowns,
　Sobriety.

If such by chance are lurking
　Let them be shown the door;
He who good wine is shirking,
　Is one of us no more.
A death's head is his face to us,
　If he abide.
Who cannot keep the pace with us,
　As well he died.

Cum contingat te prestare,
 ita bibas absque pare,
ut non possis pede stare,
neque recta verba dare,
sed sit tibi salutare
  potissimum
semper vas evacuare
  quam maximum.

Dea deo ne iungatur,
deam deus aspernatur,
nam qui Liber appellatur
libertate gloriatur,
virtus eius adnullatur
  in poculis,
et vinum debilitatur
  in copulis.

Cum regina sit in mari,
dea potest appellari,
sed indigna tanto pari,
quem presumat osculari.
numquam Bacchus adaquari
  se voluit,
nec se Liber baptizari
  sustinuit.

Should any take upon him
  To drink without a peer,
Although his legs go from him,
  His speech no longer clear,
Still for his reputation
  Let him drink on,
And swig for his salvation
  The bumper down.

But between god and goddess,
  Let there no marriage be,
For he whose name is Liber
  Exults in liberty.
Let none his single virtue
  Adulterate,
Wine that is wed with water is
  Emasculate.

Queen of the sea we grant her,
  Goddess without demur,
But to be bride to Bacchus
  Is not for such as her.
For Bacchus drinking water
  Hath no man seen;
Nor ever hath his godship
  Baptized been.

MS. OF BENEDICTBEUERN

Vagans loquitur

1

FAS et Nefas ambulant
pene passu pari;
prodigus non redimit
vitium avari;
virtus temperantia
quadam singulari
debet medium
ad utrumque vitium
caute contemplari.

2

Si legisse memoras
ethicam Catonis,
in qua scriptum legitur:
" ambula cum bonis,"
cum ad dandi gloriam
animum disponis
supra cetera
primum hoc considera,
quis sit dignus donis.

MS. OF BENEDICTBEUERN

The grace of giving

Right and wrong they go about
   Cheek by jowl together.
Lavishness can't keep in step
   Avarice his brother.
Virtue, even in the most
   Unusual moderation,
Seeking for the middle course,
   Vice on either side it, must
Look about her with the most
   Cautious contemplation.

You'll remember to have read
   In the works of Cato,
Where it plainly is set forth
   " Walk but with the worthy."
If then you have set your mind
   On the grace of giving,
This of first importance is,
   He who now your debtor is,
Can he be regarded as
   Worthily receiving?

3

Dare, non ut convenit,
non est a virtute,
bonum est secundum quid,
sed non absolute;
digne dare poteris
et mereri tute
famam muneris
si me prius noveris
intus et in cute. . . . . .

Giving otherwise is but
   Virtue by repute,
Naught but relatively good,
   Not the absolute.
But would you be generous
   With security,
Have your glory on account,
   Value full with each amount,
Hesitate no more, but give
   What you have to me.

MS. OF BENEDICTBEUERN

Dic Christi Veritas,
dic cara raritas,
dic rara Caritas,
ubi nunc habitas?
aut in valle Visionis,
aut in throno Pharaonis,
aut in alto cum Nerone,
aut in antro cum Timone,
vel in viscella scirpea
cum Moyse plorante,
vel in domo Romulea
cum bulla fulminante?

Bulla fulminante
sub iudice tonante,
reo appellante,
sententia gravante,
Veritas opprimitur,
distrahitur et venditur,
Iustitia prostante.
itur et recurritur
ad Curiam, nec ante
quis quid consequitur,
donec exuitur
ultimo quadrante.

MS. OF BENEDICTBEUERN

O TRUTH of Christ,
O most dear rarity,
O most rare Charity,
Where dwell'st thou now?
In the valley of Vision?
On Pharaoh's throne?
On high with Nero?
With Timon alone?
In the bulrush ark
Where Moses wept?
Or in Rome's high places
With lightning swept?

With the lightning of Bulls,
And a thundering judge,
Summoned, accused,
Truth stands oppressed,
Torn asunder and sold,
While Justice sells her body in the street
Come and go and come again
To the Curia, and when
Stripped to the last farthing, then
Leave the judgment seat.

Respondit Caritas;
homo, quid dubitas,
quid me sollicitas?
non sum quod usitas
nec in euro nec in austro,
nec in foro nec in claustro,
nec in bysso nec in cuculla,
nec in bello nec in bulla.
de Iericho sum veniens,
ploro cum sauciato,
quem duplex Levi transiens
non astitit grabato.

Then Love replied,
" Man, wherefore didst thou doubt? "
Not where thou wast wont to find
My dwelling in the southern wind;
Not in court and not in cloister,
Not in casque nor yet in cowl,
Not in battle nor in Bull,
But on the road from Jericho
I come with a wounded man."

MS. OF BENEDICTBEUERN

VERITAS veritatum,
via, vita, veritas!
per veritatis semitas
eliminans peccatum;
te verbum incarnatum
clamant fides, spes, caritas;
tu prime pacis statum
reformas post reatum;
tu post carnis delicias
    das gratias
    ut facias
       beatum.
o quam mira potentia,
    quam regia
    vox principis,
cum egrotanti precipis
" surge, tolle grabatum! "

MS. OF BENEDICTBEUERN

TRUTH of all truth,
O Life, O Truth, O Way,
Who by the strait paths of Thy Truth
Drivest our sin beyond the threshold of our door,
To thee, Incarnate Word,
Faith, Hope, and Charity
Continually do cry.

Thou Who dost set Thy prisoner at Thy bar, and then
Makest him a man again,
And for that forespent carnal ecstasy,
Givest such grace,
That he accounts him blessed.
O miracle of strength!
O kingly word,
That once a sick man heard,
" Arise, take up thy bed, and go thy way."

MS. OF BENEDICTBEUERN

OMNE genus demoniorum,
cecorum, claudorum, sive confusorum,
attendite iussum meorum
et vocationem verborum.

Omnis creatura phantasmatum
que corroboratis principatum
serpentis tortuosi,
venenosi,
qui traxit per superbiam
stellarum partem tertiam,
Gordan,
Ingordin et Ingordan,
per sigillum Salomonis,
et per magos Pharaonis,
omnes vos coniuro,
omnes exorcizo,
per tres magos Caspar,
Melchior et Balthasar,
per regem David,
qui Saul sedavit,
cum iubilavit,
vosque fugavit.

Vos attestor,
vos contestor,
per mandatum Domini,
ne zeletis,
quem soletis
vos vexare, homini,
ut compareatis
et post discedatis,
et cum desperatis
chaos incolatis.

MS. OF BENEDICTBEUERN

Every one of demon race,
Blind and halt and ruinous,
Hear and give ear:

Every phantom creature, ye
Who hold the principality
Of that twisted venomed snake
Who drew with him in his proud wake
One third part of heaven's stars,
Gordan,
Ingordin and Ingordan,
By the seal of Solomon,
By king Pharaoh's wise enchanters,
By the names of the Wise Men,
Caspar, Melchior, Balthasar,
By David who gave peace to Saul,
And harping banished forth you all,

I summon you and bind you
  By the will of God,
All malice leave behind you,
  And show yourselves abroad
Unto the men that ye were wont to harry.
  Once appear and then
  To Chaos get you gone,
And with all desperate things for ever tarry.

Attestor,
contestor,
per timendum,
per tremendum
diem iudicii,
eterni supplicii,
diem miserie,
perennis tristitie,
qui ducturus est
vos in infernum,
salvaturus est
nos in aeternum.

Per nomen mirabile
atque ineffabile
Dei tetragrammaton,
ut expaveatis
et perhorreatis;
vos exorcizo, Larve, Fauni, Manes,
Nymphe, Sirene, Hamadryades,
Satyri, Incubi, Penates.
ut cito abeatis,
chaos in colatis,
ne vas corrumpatis
christianitatis.

Tu nos, Deus, conservare ab hostibus digneris.

I summon you and bind you
    By that tremendous day,
The day of dread and judgment,
    Of pain eternally,
Wailing and misery,
The day of your damnation,
    And our eterne salvation.

By that unspoken name of dread
    The Tetragrammaton of God,
Let you tremble, let you groan.
I exorcise you, Ghosts and Fauns,
Goblins, Sirens, Nymphs, and Dryads,
Satyrs, Nightmares, Household Gods,
Swift to Chaos get you gone,
And no more trouble Christendom.

And do Thou, O God, vouchsafe to keep us from our foes.

MS. OF BENEDICTBEUERN

OBMITTAMUS studia,
dulce est desipere,
et carpamus dulcia
iuventutis tenere,
res est apta senectuti
seriis intendere.
Velox etas preterit
studio detenta,
lascivire suggerit
tenera iuventa.

Ver etatis labitur,
hiemps nostra properat
vita dampnum patitur,
cura carnem macerat,
sanguis aret, hebet pectus,
minuuntur gaudia,
nos deterret iam senectus
morborum familia.
Velox etas preterit
studio detenta,
lascivire suggerit
tenera iuventa.

MS. OF BENEDICTBEUERN

LET's away with study,
  Folly's sweet.
Treasure all the pleasure
  Of our youth:
Time enough for age
  To think on Truth.
So short a day,
And life so quickly hasting
And in study wasting
  Youth that would be gay!

'Tis our spring that slipping,
  Winter draweth near,
  Life itself we're losing,
  And this sorry cheer
Dries the blood and chills the heart,
  Shrivels all delight.
Age and all its crowd of ills
  Terrifies our sight.
So short a day,
And life so quickly hasting,
And in study wasting
  Youth that would be gay!

Imitemur superos!
digna est sententia,
et amoris teneros
iam venantur otia;
voto nostro serviamus,
mos iste est iuvenum,
ad plateas descendamus,
et choreas virginum.
Velox etas preterit
studio detenta,
lascivire suggerit
tenera iuventa.

Ibi que fit facilis
est videndi copia,
ibi fulget mobilis
membrorum lascivia,
dum puelle se movendo
gestibus lasciviunt,
asto videns, et videndo
me mihi subripiunt.
Velox etas preterit
studio detenta,
lascivire suggerit
tenera iuventa.

Let us as the gods do,
　'Tis the wiser part:
Leisure and love's pleasure
　Seek the young in heart
Follow the old fashion,
　Down into the street!
Down among the maidens,
　And the dancing feet!
So short a day,
And life so quickly hasting,
And in study wasting
　Youth that would be gay!

There for the seeing
　Is all loveliness,
White limbs moving
　Light in wantonness.
Gay go the dancers,
　I stand and see,
Gaze, till their glances
　Steal myself from me.
So short a day,
And life so quickly hasting,
And in study wasting
　Youth that would be gay!

MS. OF BENEDICTBEUERN

TERRA iam pandit gremium
vernali lenitate,
quod gelu triste clauserat
brumali feritate;
dulci venit strepitu
favonius cum vere,
sevum spirans boreas
iam cessat commovere.
tam grata rerum novitas
quem patitur silere?

Nunc ergo canunt iuvenes,
nunc cantum promunt volucres;
modo ferro durior
est, quem non mollit Venus,
et saxo frigidior,
qui non est igne plenus.
pellantur nubes animi,
dum aer est serenus.

Ecce, iam vernant omnia
fructu redivivo,
pulso per temperiem
iam frigore nocivo,

MS. OF BENEDICTBEUERN

THE earth lies open breasted
    In gentleness of spring,
Who lay so close and frozen
In winter's blustering.
The northern winds are quiet,
    The west wind winnowing,
In all this sweet renewing
    How shall a man not sing?

Now go the young men singing,
    And singing every bird,
Harder is he than iron
    Whom Beauty hath not stirred.
And colder than the rocks is he
    Who is not set on fire,
When cloudless are our spirits,
    Serene and still the air.

Behold, all things are springing
    With life come from the dead,
The cold that wrought for evil
    Is routed now and fled.

tellus feta sui partus
grande decus flores
gignit odoriferos
nec non multos colores.
Catonis visis talibus
inmuterentur mores.

Fronde nemus induitur,
iam canit philomena,
cum variis coloribus
iam prata sunt amena,
spatiari dulce est
per loca nemorosa,
dulcius est carpere
lilia cum rosa,
dulcissimum est ludere
cum virgine formosa.

Verum cum mentes talia
recensent oblectamina,
sentio quod anxia
fiunt mea precordia.
si friget in qua ardeo
nec mihi vult calere,
quid tunc cantus volucrum
mihi queunt valere,
cum tunc circum precordia
iam hyems est vere.

The lovely earth hath brought to birth
   All flowers, all fragrancy.
Cato himself would soften
   At such sweet instancy.

The woods are green with branches
   And sweet with nightingales,
With gold and blue and scarlet
   All flowered are the dales.
Sweet it is to wander
   In a place of trees,
Sweeter to pluck roses
   And the fleur-de-lys,
But dalliance with a lovely lass
   Far surpasseth these.

And yet when all men's spirits
   Are dreaming on delight,
My heart is heavy in me,
   And troubled at her sight:
If she for whom I travail
   Should still be cold to me,
The birds sing unavailing,
   'Tis winter still for me.

MS. OF BENEDICTBEUERN

CEDIT, hyems, tua durities,
frigor abiit; rigor et glacies
brumalis et feritas, rabies,
torpor et improba segnities,
pallor et ira, dolor et macies.

Veris adest elegans acies,
clara nitet sine nube dies,
nocte micant Pliadum facies;
grata datur modo temperies,
temporis optima mollities.

Nunc amor aureus advenies,
indomitos tibi subjicies.
tendo manus; mihi quid facies?
quam dederas rogo concilies,
et dabitur saliens aries. . . . .

MS. OF BENEDICTBEUERN

Now, Winter, yieldeth all thy dreariness,
The cold is over, all thy frozenness,
All frost and fog, and wind's untowardness.
All sullenness, uncomely sluggishness,
Paleness and anger, grief and haggardness.

Comes now the spring with all her fair arrays,
Never a cloud to stain the shining days;
Sparkle at night the starry Pleiades.
Now is the time come of all graciousness,
Now is the fairest time of gentilesse.

Now Love, all golden, comest thou to me,
Bowing the tameless neath thine empery.
I stretch my hands: what will I have of thee?
Whom thou hast given, make soft her heart to me,
And a ram leaping will I give to thee.

MS. OF BENEDICTBEUERN

IAMIAM rident prata,
iamiam virgines
iocundantur, terre
ridet facies.
estas nunc apparuit,
ornatusque florum lete claruit.

Nemus revirescit,
frondent frutices,
hiems seva cessit:
leti iuvenes,
congaudete floribus,
amor vos allicit iam virginibus.

Ergo militemus
simul Veneri,
tristia vitemus,
nos qui teneri,
visus et colloquia,
spes amorque trahant nos ad gaudia.

MS. OF BENEDICTBEUERN

Now the fields are laughing,
  Now the maidens playing,
The face of earth is smiling,
  Summer now appearing,
Joyous and lovely with all flowers beguiling.

The trees again are green,
Budding the underwood,
And cruel winter passes.
O lads, be gay of mood,
For Love himself now leads you to the lasses.

For the love of Venus
  Go we now to war,
Banish we all sadness,
  We who tender are,
And may lovely faces and soft speeches,
  Love and Hope now bring us into gladness!

MS. OF BENEDICTBEUERN

LETABUNDUS rediit
avium concentus,
ver jocundum prodiit,
gaudeat iuventus,
nova ferens gaudia;
modo vernant omnia,
Phebus serenatur,
redolens temperiem,
novo flore faciem
Flora renovatur.

Risu Jovis pellitur
torpor hiemalis,
altius extollitur
cursus estivalis
solis beneficio,
qui sublato bravio
recipit teporem.
Sic ad instar temporis
nostri Venus pectoris
reficit ardorem.

Estivant nunc Dryades,
colle sub umbroso
prodeunt Oreades,
cetu glorioso,
Satyrorum concio

MS. OF BENEDICTBEUERN

JOYOUSLY return again
   Singing-birds in chorus,
Spring is in our ways again,
   New delight before us.
   O youth, be gay!
   Green is on every spray,
   And April, sweet of breath,
   The old earth garnisheth.

Sluggish winter far away
   Clearer skies have driven,
Higher swings the summer sun
   In the arch of heaven.
   Gone is the rime,
   And come the warmer clime.
      And even so
   Love in our hearts again
   Kindles the ancient flame.

Basking are the Dryads
   In the forest rides,
Wander the Oreads
   On the green hillsides,
   Satyrs dancing,

psallit cum tripudio
Tempe per amena,
his alludens concinit,
cum iocundi meminit
veris, filomena.

Estas ab exilio
redit exoptata,
picto redit gremio
tellus purpurata,
miti cum susurrio
suo domicilio
gryllus delectatur;
et canore, iubilo,
multiformi sibilo
nemus gloriatur.

Applaudamus igitur
rerum novitati.
felix qui diligitur
voti compos grati,
dono letus Veneris,
cuius ara teneris
floribus odorat.
miser e contrario
qui sublato bravio
sine spe laborat.

Through lovely Tempe chanting,
    And through the rout,
Sings Philomel, remembering
The gladness of an older spring.

From exile comes again
    Summer the long-desired,
The earth is gay again,
    And scarlet-tired.
    Grasshopper sings
    With tiny chirrupings,
        Happy in his small house.
    With pipe and chirp and throstle
    The green wood rings.

Then let us praise together
    This earth that is new-stirred,
And happy be the lover
    Who knows his prayer is heard,
    By grace of Her
    Whose altars fragrant are
        With flowers new blown.
    And God have pity on the sadder folk,
    Who travail without hope!

MS. OF BENEDICTBEUERN

Ab estatis foribus
amor nos salutat,
humus picta floribus
faciem conmutat.
flores amoriferi
iam arrident tempori,
perit absque Venere
flos etatis tenere.

Omnium principium
dies est vernalis,
vere mundus celebrat
diem sui natalis.
omnes huius temporis
dies festi Veneris.
regna Jovis omnia
hec agant solemnia.

MS. OF BENEDICTBEUERN

At the gates of Summer,
   Love standeth us to greet,
The earth, to do him honour,
   Burgeons beneath his feet.
The flowers that aye attend him
   Laugh at the golden prime,
Should Venus not befriend them,
   They die before their time.

Of all things the beginning
   Was on an April morn,
In spring the earth remembereth
   The day that she was born.
And so the feast of Venus,
   Wherever Jove holds sway,
By mortal and Immortal,
   Is kept a holiday.

MS. OF BENEDICTBEUERN

ESTAS non apparuit
  preteritis temporibus
que sic clara fuerit;
  ornantur prata floribus.
    Aves nunc in silva canunt
    et canendo dulce garriunt.

Iuno Iovem superat
  amore maritali,
Mars a Vulcano capitur
  re artificiali.
    Aves nunc in silva canunt . . .

In exemplum Veneris
  hec fabula proponitur,
Phebus Daphnem sequitur,
  Europa tauro luditur.
    Aves nunc in silva canunt . . .

Amor querit iuvenes
  ut ludant cum virginibus,
Venus despicit senes,
  qui inpleti sunt doloribus.
    Aves nunc in silva canunt . . .

MS. OF BENEDICTBEUERN

NEVER ancient summer
   In the ancient days
So fair as this late comer
   In her flowering ways.
Down in the greenwood sing the birds.

Dame Juno hath reconquered
   The sire of gods and men,
Vulcan hath taken in his net
   Beauty and War again.
Down in the greenwood sing the birds.

With glory of the goddess
   Are the old legends full,
Of Daphne and Apollo,
   Europa and the Bull.
Down in the greenwood sing the birds.

It is for youth, youth only,
   To love, be loved again.
For beauty mocks at old men,
   The old are full of pain.
Down in the greenwood sing the birds.

MS. OF BENEDICTBEUERN

Tempus est iocundum,
o virgines,
modo congaudete
vos iuvenes

> *O. o. totus floreo,*
> *iam amore virginali*
> *totus ardeo,*
> *novus novus amor*
> *est, quo pereo.*

Cantat philomena
sic dulciter,
et modulans auditur;
intus caleo
O. o. totus floreo . . .

MS. OF BENEDICTBEUERN

New love

Now's the time for pleasure,
  Lads and lasses,
Take your joy together
  Ere it passes.
With the love of a maid
  Aflower,
With the love of a maid
  Afire,
New love, new love,
  Dying of desire.

Philomel singing
  So sweet,
My heart burns to hear her
  Repeat,
With the love of a maid
  Aflower,
With the love of a maid
  Afire,
New love, new love,
  Dying of desire.

Flos est puellarum,
quam diligo,
et rosa rosarum,
quam sepe video;
   O. o. totus floreo . . .

Tua me confortat
promissio,
tua me deportat
negatio.
   O. o. totus floreo . . .

Tua mecum ludit
virginitas,
tua me detrudit
simplicitas.
   O. o. totus floreo . . .

Flower of all maidens,
  My love,
Rose o'er all roses
  Above.
With the love of a maid
  Aflower,
With the love of a maid
  Afire,
New love, new love,
  Dying of desire.

All the sweet of life,
  Thy consenting,
All the bitterness,
  Thy repenting.
With the love of a maid
  Aflower,
With the love of a maid
  Afire,
New love, new love,
  Dying of desire.

Thy virginity
  Mocks my wooing,
Thy simplicity
  Is my undoing.
With the love of a maid
  Aflower,
With the love of a maid
  Afire,
New love, new love,
  Dying of desire.

Sile, philomena,
pro tempore,
surge cantilena
de pectore.
  O. o. totus floreo . . .

Tempore brumali
vir patiens,
animo vernali
lasciviens.
  O. o. totus floreo . . .

Veni, domicella,
cum gaudio,
veni, veni, bella,
iam pereo.
  O. o. totus floreo,
  iam amore virginali
  totus ardeo,
  novus novus amor
  est, quo pereo.

O nightingale, be still
  For an hour,
Till the heart sings,
With the love of a maid
  Aflower,
With the love of a maid
  Afire,
New love, new love,
  Dying of desire.

Patient I have been,
  Winter long,
Now comes wanton spring
  With a song.
With the love of a maid
  Aflower,
With the love of a maid
  Afire,
New love, new love,
  Dying of desire.

Come, mistress mine,
  Joy with thee,
Come, fairest, come,
  Love, to me.
With the love of a maid
  Aflower,
With the love of a maid
  Afire,
New love, new love,
  Dying of desire.

MS. OF BENEDICTBEUERN

VOLO virum vivere viriliter,
diligam, si diligar equaliter.
sic amandum censeo, non aliter.
hac in parte fortior quam Jupiter
nescio precari
commercio vulgari;
amaturus forsitan
volo prius amari.

Mulieris animi superbiam
gravi supercilio despiciam,
nec maiorem terminum subiciam,
neque bubus aratrum preficiam;
displicet hic usus
in miseros diffusus;
malo plaudens ludere
quam plangere delusus.

Que cupit ut placeat, huic placeam;
prius ipsa faveat, ut faveam:
non ludemus aliter hanc aleam,
ne se granum reputet, me paleam;
pari lege fori
deserviam amori,
ne prosternar impudens
femineo pudori.

MS. OF BENEDICTBEUERN

I WOULD have a man live in manly fashion.
Yea, I shall love, but given an equal passion:
So to my mind should love be,
And no other,
And herein myself I see
A better man than Jupiter.
I know not how to pray
In the old vulgar way.
Would she have me love her?
Then shall she first love me.

Well do I know the pride of woman's spirit,
And with sardonic eyebrow I contemn it.
Shall I put the greater last?
Set the ox behind the plough?
This common guise
Of wretches I despise,
And rather choose myself to play
Than be the toy that's thrown away.

She who fain would please me, I shall please,
First shall she show her favour, for returning.
So shall we throw the main,
She shall not think me chaff,
Herself the grain.
I shall Love's servant be,
But with an equal yoke for her and me,
I'll have no woman laugh
At me flung prostrate by her coyness spurning.

229

Liber ego liberum me iactito
casto fore similem Hippolyto;
non me vincit mulier tam subito
que seducat oculis ac digito.
dicat me placere,
et diligat sincere;
hoc mihi protervitas
placet in muliere.

Ecce, mihi displicet quod cecini,
et meo contrarius sum carmini,
tue reus, domina, dulcedini,
cuius elegantie non memini.
quia sic erravi,
sum dignus pena gravi;
penitentem corripe,
si placet, in conclavi.

Free am I, and I boast myself as free.
Hippolytus was chaste, I chaste as he.
Nor with sudden wooing
Shall she be my undoing,
Tender eyes and hands seducing.
Let her pleasure in me find,
Love me most sincerely.
This forwardness towards me designed
Pleases in the female mind.

Alas, alas, what is it I have sung?
My song was all a lie, I am undone,
Lady, thy prisoner I!
Thy loveliness forgot,
Thy sweetness heeded not,
Worthy am I of all thy cruelty.
I do confess my guilt,
Then chide me as thou wilt,
But let thy chamber my tribunal be.

MS. OF BENEDICTBEUERN

SALVE ver optatum,
amantibus gratum,
gaudiorum
fax multorum,
florum incrementum;
multitudo florum
et color colorum
salvetote,
et estote
iocorum augmentum!
Dulcis avium concentus
sonat, gaudeat iuventus.
hiems seva transiit,
nam lenis spirat ventus.

Tellus purpurata
floribus et prata
revirescunt,
umbre crescunt,
nemus redimitur.
lascivit natura
omnis creatura;
leto vultu,
claro cultu,
ardor investitur;
Venus subditos titillat,
dum nature nectar stillat
sic ardor venereus
amantibus scintillat. . . . .

MS. OF BENEDICTBEUERN

O Spring the long-desired,
  The lover's hour!
O flaming torch of joy,
Sap of each flower,
  All hail!
O jocund company
  Of many flowers,
O many-coloured light,
  All hail,
And foster our delight!
The birds sing out in chorus,
O youth, joy is before us,
Cold winter has passed on,
And the spring winds are come!

The earth's aflame again
  With flowers bright,
The fields are green again,
  The shadows deep,
Woods are in leaf again,
There is no living thing
That is not gay again.
  With face of light,
  Garbed with delight,
  Love is reborn,
And Beauty wakes from sleep.

MS. OF BENEDICTBEUERN

ECCE, chorus virginum,
   tempore vernali,
dum solis incendium
   radios equali
moderatur ordine,
   iubilo semoto,
fronde pausa tilie
   Cypridis in voto!
     Cypridis in voto!
     Fronde pausa tilie
      Cypridis in voto!

In hac valle florida
   floreus, fragratus,
intra septa lilia
   locus purpuratus.
dum garritus merule
   dulciter alludit.
philomena carmine
   dulcia concludit.

MS. OF BENEDICTBEUERN

HERE be maids dancing
  In the spring days,
April light lancing
  Long level rays.
Peace to your piping!
  With linden boughs
At Beauty's altar
  Pay ye your vows!
With linden boughs
  At Beauty's altar
Pay ye your vows!

In this fair valley,
  Fragrant and sweet,
Is a bright alley
  With lilies deep,
Where the gay blackbird
  Pipes all day long,
Sweetness recordeth
  The nightingale's song.
With linden boughs
  At Beauty's altar
Pay ye your vows!

Acies virginea
    redimita flore;
quis enarret talia,
    quantoque decore
prenitent ad libitum
    Veneris occulta!
Dido necis meritum
    proferat inulta. . . . .

Here come the virgins
  Flower-garlanded,
But who shall sing them,
  How shall be said
That blaze of beauty,
  Love's secret store?
Tales of old sorrow
  Grieve us no more.
With linden boughs
  At Beauty's altar
Pay ye your vows !

MS. OF BENEDICTBEUERN

MUSA venit carmine,
dulci modulamine:
pariter cantemus,
ecce virent omnia,
prata, rus et nemus,
mane garrit alaudula,
lupilulat cornicula,
iubente natura
philomena queritur
antiqua de iactura.

Hirundo iam finsat,
cignus dulce trinsat
memorando fata,
cuculat et cuculus
per nemora vernata.

Pulchre canunt volucres,
nitet terre facies
vario colore,
et in partum solvitur
redolens odore.

MS. OF BENEDICTBEUERN

GAY comes the singer
  With a song,
Sing we all together,
  All things young;
Field and wood and fallow,
  Lark at dawn,
Young rooks cawing, cawing,
  Philomel
Still complaining of the ancient wrong.

Twitters now the swallow,
  Swans are shrill
Still remembering sorrow,
Cuckoo, cuckoo, goes the cuckoo calling
  On the wooded hill.

The birds sing fair,
  Shining earth,
Gracious after travail
  Of new birth,
Lies in radiant light,
  Fragrant air.

Late pandit tilia
frondes, ramos, folia,
thymus est sub ea,
viridi cum gramine,
in quo fit chorea.

Patet et in gramine
iocundo rivus murmure.
locus est festivus,
ventus cum temperie
susurrat tempestivus.

Broad spreads the lime,
　Bough and leaf.
Underfoot the thyme,
　Green the turf.
Here come the dances,
　In the grass
Running water glances,
　Murmurs past.

Happy is the place,
　Whispering.
Through the open weather
　Blow the winds of spring.

MS. OF BENEDICTBEUERN

CLAUSUS Chronos et serato
carcere ver exit,
risu Jovis reserato
faciem detexit,
purpurato
floret prato.
ver tene primatum
ex algenti
renitenti
specie renatum.

Vernant veris ad amena
—thyma, rosa, lilia,
his alludit filomena,
melos et lascivia.

Satyrus hoc excitatur,
et Dryadum chorea,
redivivis incitatur
hoc ignibus Napea.

o Cupido, concitus
hoc amor innovatur,
hoc ego sollicitus,
hoc mihi mens turbatur.

MS. OF BENEDICTBEUERN

Time's shut up and Spring
Hath broken prison,
Into clearer skies
Hath the sun arisen,
Purple flowers the heath.
Spring, put thy kingship on,
Reborn to gleaming beauty
From frozen earth.

Now springs the thyme in all his pleasant places,
    Roses and fleur-de-lys,
And Philomel sweet singing
    In wanton melody.

The Satyrs are awake,
    Dancing the Dryads,
The nymphs in the brake
    Kindling for his sake,
        Lit with new fires.

O Love, by Spring awakened,
    Desire is born,
And by the spring-fret shaken,
    My mind is torn.

Ignem alo tacitum,
amo, nec ad placitum,
utquid contra libitum
cupio prohibitum,
votis Venus meritum
rite facit irritum,
trudit in interitum
quem rebar emeritum.

Si quis amans per amare
amari posset mereri,
posset amor mihi velle mederi,
quod facile sit, tandem beare,
perdo querelas absque levare.

Hoc amor predicat,
hec macilenta
hoc sibi vendicat
absque perempta . . .

Parce dato pia
Cypris agone,
et quia vincimur,
arma repone,
et quibus es Venus,
esto Dione.

I love, to my undoing,
  The flame I tend is hidden,
And dangerous my wooing,
  Desire of the forbidden.
My goddess in her wisdom
  Makes naught of my poor vows,
And draws unto his ruin
One broken in her wars.

And yet, if ever lover
  By loving love might earn,
Love might me yet recover,
  And at the last might turn
And bid me happiness,
For these complaints that lighten not distress.

For this is Love's own hour,
  This wretchedness
He claims in his own power,
  Without redress.

O gracious Cyprian,
  Have pity now.
Have I not borne enough?
  Lay down thy bow!
Yea, thou hast conquered, lay
  Thy weapons down.
Thou hast been Beauty, thou hast been Desire:
  Be Love alone.

MS. OF BENEDICTBEUERN

NOBILIS, mei
miserere precor,
tua facies
ensis est quo necor,
nam medullitus
amat meum te cor,
subveni!
Amor improbus
omnia superat,
subveni !

Come sperulas
tue eliciunt
cordi sedulas,
flammas adjiciunt,
hebet animus,
vires deficiunt:
subveni!
Amor improbus
omnia superat,
subveni !

MS. OF BENEDICTBEUERN

Noblest, I pray thee

Noblest, I pray thee,
Have pity upon me,
Thy face is a sword,
And behold, I am slain.
From the core of my heart I have loved thee,
Aid, oh aid!
Love the deceiver,
Love the all-conquering,
Come to mine aid !

Thy hair hath entangled
My very heart's fibre.
The flame is upleaping,
And sinking my soul.
All strength ebbs from me,
Aid, oh aid!
Love the deceiver,
Love the all-conquering,
Come to mine aid !

Odor roseus
spirat a labiis;
speciosior
pre cunctis filiis,
melle dulcior,
pulchrior liliis,
subveni!
Amor improbus
omnia superat,
subveni !

Decor prevalet
candori etheris;
ad pretorium
presentor Veneris;
ecce pereo,
si non subveneris;
subveni!
Amor improbus
omnia superat,
subveni !

The breath of red roses
Is thy lips breathing,
Lovelier art thou
Than all the world's maidens,
Sweeter than honey and whiter than lilies.
Aid, oh aid!
Love the deceiver,
Love the all-conquering,
Come to mine aid !

Thy beauty distaineth
The shining of heaven,
At the temple of Venus
I suppliant stand.
Behold, for I perish, if thou wilt not aid me!
Aid, oh aid!
Love the deceiver,
Love the all-conquering,
Come to mine aid !

MS. OF BENEDICTBEUERN

PRATA iam rident omnia,
dulce est flores carpere,
sed nox donat his somnia,
qui semper vellent ludere:
ve ve miser, quid faciam?
Venus, mihi subvenias,
tuam iam colo gratiam.

Plangit cor meum misere,
quia caret solatio.
si velles hoc cognoscere,
bene posses, ut sentio.
o tu virgo pulcherrima,
si non audis me miserum,
mihi mors est asperrima.

Tempus accedit floridum,
hiemps discedit temere,
omne quod fuit aridum,
germen suum vult gignere;
quamdiu modo vixeris,
semper letare, iuvenis,
quia nescis cum deperis.

Dulcis appares omnibus,
sed es mihi dulcissima,
tu pre cunctis virginibus
incedis ut castissima,
o tu, mitis considera,
nam per te gemitus
passus sum et suspiria.

MS. OF BENEDICTBEUERN

O SWEET are flowers to gather,
  The meadows laugh to-day,
But night brings too much dreaming
  To some who still would play.
O sorrow on me, what am I to do?
O Lady Venus, wilt thou have no rue
  On him who seeks thy grace?

My heart's for ever grieving
  And is not comforted.
If thou wert but believing,
  Then were I lightly sped.
O maid most lovely fair,
If thou wilt have no care,
  Then, cruel, am I dead.

Sudden is winter gone,
  The time is blossoming,
And all that barren was
  Is burgeoning.
O Youth, while life is with thee,
Take thou delight unto thee,
  Thou knowest not thy dying.

Sweet dost thou seem to all,
  But sweeter far to me,
Above all maids that are,
  Thou walk'st in chastity.
Bethink thee, gentle heart,
For thee is all my smart,
  And my sore sighing.

251

MS. OF BENEDICTBEUERN

Suscipe Flos florem,
　quia flos designat amorem.
illo de flore
　nimio sum captus amore.
hunc florem, Flora
　dulcissima, semper odora,
nam velut aurora
　fiet tua forma decora.
florem Flora vide,
　quem dum videas, mihi ride.
florem Flora tene,
　tua vox cantus philomene.
oscula des flori,
　rubeo flos convenit ori.
flos in pictura
　non est flos, immo figura;
qui pingit florem
　non pingit floris odorem.

MS. OF BENEDICTBEUERN

Take thou this rose

TAKE thou this rose, O Rose,
  Since Love's own flower it is,
And by that rose
  Thy lover captive is.

Smell thou this rose, O Rose,
And know thyself as sweet
As dawn is sweet.

Look on this rose, O Rose,
And looking, laugh on me,
And in thy laughter's ring
The nightingale shall sing.

Kiss thou this rose, O Rose,
That it may know the scarlet of thy mouth.

O Rose, this painted rose
  Is not the whole,
Who paints the flower
  Paints not its fragrant soul.

253

MS. OF BENEDICTBEUERN

O COMES amoris dolor,
cuius mala male solor,
nec habent remedium,
dolor urget me, nec mirum,
quem a predilecta dirum
en vocat exilium,
cuius laus est singularis,
pro qua non curasset Paris
Helene consortium.

Gaude vallis insignita,
vallis rosis redimita,
vallis flos convallium,
inter valles vallis una,
quam collaudat sol et luna,
dulcis cantus avium,
quam collaudat philomena.
nam quam dulcis et amena
mestis dans solatium!

MS. OF BENEDICTBEUERN

O Sorrow, that art still Love's company,
Whose griefs abide with me,
And have no remedy,
Sorrow doth drive me: how else should it be?
I go to exile from my darling one;
There is none like her, none,
Had Paris seen her, Helen were alone.

O valley, still be gay,
Valley with roses climbing all the way,
Among all valleys one,
Valley the fairest that is in the hills.
Soft on thee shines the sun,
Softly the moon; the birds
Sing rare for thee. O valley, be thou fair!
Yea, for the sick at heart find solace there.

MS. OF BENEDICTBEUERN

ANNI novi rediit novitas,
hiemis cedit asperitas,
breves dies prolongantur,
elementa temperantur.
subintrante Januario
mens estu languet vario,
propter puellam quam diligo.

Prudens est multumque formosa
pulchrior lilio vel rosa,
gracili coartatur statura,
prestantior omni creatura,
placet plus Francie regina.
mihi mors est iam vicina,
nisi sanet me flos de spina.

Venus me telo vulneravit
aureo, quod cor penetravit.
Cupido faces instillavit,
Amor amorem superavit
iuvencule pro qua volo mori.
non iungar cariori,
licet accrescat dolor dolori.

Illius captus sum amore,
cuius flos adhuc est in flore.
dulcis fit labor in hoc labore,
osculum si sumat os ab ore.
non tactu sanabor labiorum,
nisi cor unum fiat duorum
et idem velle. Vale, flos florum!

MS. OF BENEDICTBEUERN

New Year

NEW Year has brought renewing, winter's gone,
Short daylight lengthens and the winds are still,
The year's first month of January's here,
And in my mind the tides still ebb and flow
     For a girl's sake.

Slenderly fashioned is she, wise and fair,
Lovelier than the lily or the rose.
The Queen of France is not so beautiful.
And Death is now near neighbour unto me
Unless she heal the wound she made in me,
     Flower o' the thorn.

Beauty hath pierced me with her golden shaft,
Cupid had kindled me, love upon love,
This little maid, for whom I'd gladly die.
No dearer heart, though for her love have I
     Grief upon grief.

Thus captive am I for the love of her
Whose flower is newly blown.
O sweet should be the travail of that hour,
If ever on her mouth my mouth were sealed!
Yet never by her mouth could I be healed,
Unless upon my heart her heart were still,
     Her will my will.
Rose of all roses, hail!

MS. OF BENEDICTBEUERN

DIRA vi amoris teror,
et venereo axe vehor,
igne ferventi suffocatus.
deme, pia, cruciatus.

Ignis vivi tu scintilla,
discurrens cordis ad vexilla;
igni incumbens non pauxillo
conclusi mentis te sigillo.

Meret cor, quod gaudebat;
die, quo te cognoscebat,
singularem et pudicam
te adoptabat in amicam.

Profert pectoris singultus
et mestitie tumultus,
nam amoris tui vigor
urget me, et illi ligor.

MS. OF BENEDICTBEUERN

By the dread force of love am I thus worn,
On the wheel of desire am I thus torn,
  I stifle in the fire.
O merciful, bid thou my torment cease!

Thou spark of living fire,
Kindling the very secrets of desire,
  Bowed o'er so fierce a flame,
I set thee on my heart as with a seal.

Mourns now the heart for that which made it glad;
That day when first of thee it knowledge had,
  It chose thee for its love,
Chose thee, unsullied, none beside thee, none.

Now naught but sighing breaks forth from my breast,
Tumult of sorrow will not let me rest,
  Strong love of thee
Urges me on, and to it am I bound.

Virginale lilium,
tuum praesta subsidium.
missus in exilium
querit a te consilium.

Nescit quid agat, moritur,
amore tui vehitur,
telo necatur Veneris
sibi ne subveneris.

Iure Veneris orbata,
castitas redintegrata,
vultu decenti perornata,
veste sophie decorata,

Psallo tibi soli,
despicere me noli,
per me precor velis coli,
lucens ut stella poli.

O virgin lily, come thou to mine aid,
Thine exile prays thee to be comforted,
    He knows not what he does.
And if thou wilt not succour him, he dies.

O thou on whom Desire hath no power,
Thou in whom Chastity's reborn in flower,
    Sweet still regard,
Thou who hast truth about thee for a cloak,

I sing to thee, I sing to thee alone.
Despise him not, who asks this only boon,
    That he may worship thee,
Thou who dost shine above him like a star.

MS. OF BENEDICTBEUERN

Dᴜᴍ estas inchoatur
ameno tempore,
Phebusque dominatur
depulso frigore,

Unius in amore
puelle vulneror
multimodo dolore,
per quem et atteror.

Ut mei misereatur,
ut me recipiat,
et declinetur ad me,
et ita desinat!

MS. OF BENEDICTBEUERN

WHILE summer on is stealing,
  And come the gracious prime,
And Phœbus high in heaven,
  And fled the rime,

For love of one young maiden,
  My heart hath ta'en its wound,
And manifold the grief that I
  In love have found.

Ah, would she but have pity,
  And take me to her grace,
And stooping lean down o'er me,
  And so would rest!

MS. OF BENEDICTBEUERN

Dum Diane vitrea
sero lampas oritur,
et a fratris rosea
luce dum succenditur,
dulcis aura zephyri
spirans omnes etheri
nubes tollit;
sic emollit
vi chordarum pectora,
et inmutat
cor quod nutat
ad amoris pignora.
letum iubar hesperi
gratiorem
dat humorem
roris soporiferi
mortalium generi.

O quam felix est
antidotum soporis,
quod curarum tempestates
sedat et doloris!
dum surrepit clausis
oculorum poris,
gaudio equiparat
dulcedini amoris.

MS. OF BENEDICTBEUERN

WHEN Diana lighteth
Late her crystal lamp,
Her pale glory kindleth
From her brother's fire,
Little straying west winds
Wander over heaven,
Moonlight falleth,
And recalleth
With a sound of lute-strings shaken,
Hearts that have denied his reign
To love again.
Hesperus, the evening star,
To all things that mortal are,
Grants the dew of sleep.

Thrice happy Sleep!
The antidote to care,
Thou dost allay the storm
Of grief and sore despair;
Through the fast-closed gates
Thou stealest light;
Thy coming gracious is
As Love's delight.

Morpheus in mentem
trahit impellentem
ventum lenem
segetes maturas,
murmura rivorum
per arenas puras,
circulares ambitus
molendinorum,
qui furantur somno
lumen oculorum.

Post blanda Veneris commercia,
lassatur cerebri substantia.
hinc caligantes mira novitate,
oculi nantes in palpebrarum rate!
hei quam felix transitus amoris ad soporem,
sed suavior regressus soporis ad amorem! . . . .

Fronde sub arboris amena,
dum querens canit philomena,
suave est quiescere,
suavius ludere
in gramine
cum virgine
speciosa.
si variarum
odor herbarum
spiraverit,
si dederit
thorum rosa,
dulciter soporis alimonia
post Veneris defessa commercia
captatur
dum lassis instillatur . . . .

Sleep through the wearied brain
Breathes a soft wind
From fields of ripening grain,
The sound
Of running water over clearest sand,
A millwheel turning, turning slowly round,
These steal the light
From eyes weary of sight.

Love's sweet exchange and barter, then the brain
Sinks to repose;
Swimming in strangeness of a new delight
The eyelids close;
Oh sweet the passing o'er from love to sleep.
But sweeter the awakening to love.

Under the kind branching trees
Where Philomel complains and sings
Most sweet to lie at ease,
Sweeter to take delight
Of beauty and the night
On the fresh springing grass,
With smell of mint and thyme,
And for Love's bed, the rose.
Sleep's dew doth ever bless,
But most distilled on lovers' weariness.

MS. OF BENEDICTBEUERN

Sᴍᴄ mea fata canendo solor,
ut nece proxima facit olor.
roseus effugit ore color,
blandus inest meo cordi dolor.
    cura crescente,
    labore vigente,
    vigore labente,
    miser morior,
hei morior, hei morior, hei morior!
dum quod amem cogor, sed non amor

Si me dignetur quam desidero,
felicitate Jovem supero.
nocte cum illa si dormiero
si sua labra semel suxero,
    mortem subire,
    placenter obire,
    vitamque finire
    libens potero,
hei potero, hei potero, hei potero.
tanta si gaudia recepero.

MS. OF BENEDICTBEUERN

So by my singing am I comforted
Even as the swan that singing makes death sweet,
For from my face is gone the wholesome red,
And soft grief in my heart is sunken deep.
　　　For sorrow still increasing,
　　　And travail unreleasing,
　　　And strength from me fast flying,
　　　And I for sorrow dying,
Dying, dying, dying,
Since she I love cares nothing for my sighing.

If she whom I desire would stoop to love me,
　I should look down on Jove;
If for one night my lady would lie by me,
　And I kiss the mouth I love,
　　　Then come Death unrelenting,
　　　With quiet breath consenting,
　　　I go forth unrepenting,
Content, content, content,
That such delight were ever to me lent.

Ubera cum animadverterem
optavi manus, ut involverem,
simplicibus mammis ut alluderem
sic cogitando sensi Venerem,
      sedit in ore
      rosa cum pudore,
      pulsatus amore
      quod os lamberem,
hei lamberem, hei lamberem, hei lamberem,
luxuriando per characterem.

Innocent breasts, when I have looked upon them,
  Would that my hands were there,
How have I craved, and dreaming thus upon them,
  Love wakened from despair.
      Beauty on her lips flaming,
      Rose red with her shaming,
      And I with passion burning
      And with my whole heart yearning
For her mouth, her mouth, her mouth,
That on her beauty I might slake my drouth.

MS. OF BENEDICTBEUERN

Estas in exilium
iam peregrinatur,
leto nemus avium
cantu viduatur,
pallet viror frondium,
campus defloratur,
exaruit quod floruit,
quia felicem statum nemoris
vis frigoris
sinistra denudavit,
et ethera silentio turbavit,
exilio dum aves relegavit.

Sed amorem,
qui calorem
nutrit, nulla vis
frigoris
valet attenuare,
sed ea reformare
studet, que corruperat
brume torpor.
amare crucior, morior
vulnere, quo glorior.
eia, si me sanare
uno vellet osculo,
que cor felici iaculo
gaudet vulnerare! . . . .

MS. OF BENEDICTBEUERN

SUMMER to a strange land
  Is into exile gone,
The forest trees are bare
  Of their gay song.
The forest boughs are wan,
  Deflowered the field,
Withered that which was fair,
  Naked and bare
The happy greenwood is,
  Stripped by the cruel cold,
And silence grieves the air,
  For all the birds are into exile gone.

But upon love,
  Love that itself is fire,
No power hath the cold,
  For love's desire
Kindleth afresh that which was dead and old
In winter's hold.
  I suffer, yea, I die,
Yet this mine agony
  I count all bliss,
Since death is life again
  Upon her lips!

XIIITH CENTURY MS.

DE ramis cadunt folia,
nam viror totus periit,
iam calor liquit omnia
    et abiit;
nam signa coeli ultima
    sol petiit.

Iam nocet frigus teneris,
et avis bruma leditur,
et philomena ceteris
    conqueritur,
quod illis ignis etheris
    adimitur.

Nec lympha caret alveus,
nec prata virent herbida,
sol nostra fugit aureus
    confinia;
est inde dies niveus,
    nox frigida.

Modo frigescit quidquid est,
    sed solus ego caleo;
immo sic mihi cordi est
    quod ardeo;
hic ignis tamen virgo est,
    qua langueo.

XIIITH CENTURY MS.

Down from the branches fall the leaves,
A wanness comes on all the trees,
    The summer's done;
And into his last house in heaven
    Now goes the sun.

Sharp frost destroys the tender sprays,
Birds are a-cold in these short days.
    The nightingale
Is grieving that the fire of heaven
    Is now grown pale.

The swollen river rushes on
Past meadows whence the green has gone,
    The golden sun
Has fled our world.   Snow falls by day,
    The nights are numb.

About me all the world is stark,
And I am burning; in my heart
    There is a fire,
A living flame in me, the maid
    Of my desire.

Nutritur ignis osculo
　　et leni tactu virginis;
in suo lucet oculo
　　lux luminis,
nec est in toto seculo
　　plus numinis.

Ignis grecus extinguitur
　　cum vino iam acerrimo;
sed iste non extinguitur
　　miserrimo:
immo fomento alitur
　　uberrimo.

Her kisses, fuel of my fire,
Her tender touches, flaming higher.
    The light of light
Dwells in her eyes: divinity
    Is in her sight.

Greek fire can be extinguishèd
By bitter wine; my fire is fed
    On other meat.
Yea, even the bitterness of love
    Is bitter-sweet.

ARUNDEL MS.

Ipsa vivere   mihi reddidit!
cessit prospere,   spe plus accidit
menti misere:
que dum temere   totam tradidit
se sub Venere,
Venus ethere   risus edidit
leto sidere.

Desiderio   nimis officit,
dum vix gaudio   pectus sufficit,
quod concipio
dum Venerio   Flora reficit
me colloquio,
dum, quem haurio,   favus allicit
dato basio.

Sepe refero   cursum liberum
sinu tenero: sic me superum
addens numero.
cunctis impero,   felix iterum
si tetigero
quem desidero,   sinum tenerum
tactu libero.

ARUNDEL MS.

HERSELF hath given back my life to me,
Herself hath yielded far
More than had ever hoped my misery.
And when she recklessly
Gave herself wholly unto Love and me,
Beauty in heaven afar
Laughed from her joyous star.

Too great desire hath overwhelmed me,
My heart's not great enough
For this huge joy that overmastered me,
What time my love
Made in her arms another man of me,
And all the gathered honey of her lips
Drained in one yielded kiss.

Again, again, I dream the freedom given
Of her soft breast,
And so am come, another god, to heaven
Among the rest.
Yea, and serene would govern gods and men,
If I might find again
My hand upon her breast.

279

BIOGRAPHICAL NOTES

COPA

(Dancing Girl of Syria)

THE *Copa* belongs to that small miscellany of lighter verse that Servius attributed to Virgil in the fourth century, and that came down through the Middle Ages bobbing at a painter's end in the mighty wash of the Aeneid. His great name secured it a kind of charmed passage; and the ascription persists among lovers of Virgil still. Its closeness to the Virgilian letter and extreme remoteness from the Virgilian spirit have left it one of the riddles of authorship, and Dr. Mackail's solution is perhaps as satisfying as any: that it is so unlike Virgil he may very well have written it. For that matter, it is unlike anything else in Augustan Latin. Horace has the steady-pacing Death, even the *Vivite, ait, venio,* but not this grim humorous Death who tweaks one's ear in the by-going: Propertius has the languor of the disillusioned senses, but not its smiling virile mockery. Like the *Pervigilium Veneris* it stands solitary in literature till the *novitas rerum,* the renewing of all things, in the twelfth century. A single line from it

> *Pone merum et talos. pereat qui crastina curat!*

(Set down the wine and the dice, and perish who thinks of to-morrow!) is quoted in the *Carmina Burana,* the profane service-book of the Wandering Scholars: it might stand as motto of their vagabond order.

There is another mediæval citation of it, academic this time. Mico, master of the oblates in the monastery of

St. Riquier from 825–853, noted the line about the little
cheeses that they dry in baskets of rushes, and entered it
in his *Opus Prosodiacum* thus:

Fiscina. *Sunt et caseoli quos iuncea fiscina siccat.* Virgilivs.

He began his Dictionary of Prosody because he had taken
to heart the criticism of a scholarly visitor at the Abbey,
who said that the brethren's quantities left much to be
desired. *Vir studiosus et valde doctus*, an earnest man and
mightily learned, said John of Tritheim of him, and himself
a poet, writing small agreeable verses as inscriptions for
his cloister, on the apple-room for instance, and on a friend
who saw a vision of Bacchus as he sat on the grass, and,
this from personal experience, on the disadvantages of
stoutness in scholarship: he was interested in contem-
porary poetry as well as in the classics, for he quotes from
poets of the last generation such as Paul the Deacon, and
from young contemporaries such as Walafrid Strabo, as
well as from Virgil and—a rare thing in mediæval scholar-
ship—Lucretius.

It is probable that Mico's manuscript of the *Copa* was
brought to the Abbey in 814, when Angilbert, the greatest
among Charlemagne's princes, came there to die, while
Charlemagne himself lay dying in Aix-la-Chapelle. He
had been, in the intervals of passionate penitence that
broke his crowded life, its Abbot, though he never laid aside
his secular splendour: a great soldier, a lover of music and
books and verses—one of his own has the refrain, " My lute,
awake "—and himself so loveable that Charlemagne for-
gave him his passion for one of the fairy-tale princesses
whom no mam night marry, and the son that he had by
her, who grew up into a sober historian. Dying, he left
the Abbey his magnificent library of two hundred MSS.,
and his body to be buried, not in the great abbey church
that he had built, but beneath the pavement at the steps,

so that the feet of the brethren as they went in and out might pass above his head. Some years later, they carried his body into the church and built a tomb above it, not thinking it fitting that so great a benefactor of their Abbey should lie so low: and meantime Mico browsed among the manuscripts, and made a *hortus siccus* of the tavern garlands.

What became of the manuscript of the *Copa* that Mico used is not known: but a ninth century MS. in Lombard script, the oldest and best (Vatican 3252) once belonged to Cardinal Bembo, whose descant in praise of Platonic love transfigures the last pages of Castiglione's *Courtier*, and to whom Lucrezia Borgia wrote the little packet of letters over which Byron pored for hours in the Ambrosian library, to the scandal of the scholarly librarian who would have shown him graver documents. Bembo took a good deal of trouble with the *Copa*, and his emendation of one line, which he seems to have owed rather to his experience of Lucrezia than of palæography, has crept into many editions.

Formosum tenerae decerpens ora puellae,

read the MSS. a little obscurely:

Candida formosae decerpens ora puellae,

read the Cardinal. The text on which the present translation was first based was his, and I have been reluctant to abandon it, though to write " scarlet " for *candida*, even in its sense of " glowing," is perhaps to out-cardinal the Cardinal. The reading given in the text for *formosum* is Robinson Ellis's very ingenious " *per morsum*," " reaping by a bite," which indeed, he adds sardonically, it did not require an Œdipus to discover.

The reading *fumosa*, smoky, in line 3, instead of *famosa*, well-known, is supported by three MSS. only, the Munich group, eleventh and twelfth century. It has no prerogative: yet it accords better with the half-rustic tavern, where even a shabby donkey might be welcome, than the sophisticated *famosa* of the suburbs or the capital.

In line 14,

sertaque purpurea lutea mixta rosa,

the translation of *serta* by " melilot," rather than the conventional " garland," has been challenged. It is true that in this sense it only occurs thrice in classical Latin. Cato advises *serta campanica bene odorata*, sweet-smelling Campanian melilot, to be pounded with dry orris root, added to six measures of the best must, and simmered gently in a copper vessel over a fire of small twigs, and then smeared on the lips of wine jars for their safe keeping and sweet odour: he also uses it in his recipe for Coan wine, which begins by drawing water from a quiet sea on a day when there shall be no wind. But Pliny's use of it is more decisive: in numbering the flowers which may be used for garlands rather by virtue of their leaf than their flower, white bryony, meadowsweet, marjoram, balm-gentle, he dwells longest upon " melilot, which we call *sertulam Campanam*." For, he adds, " it is much beloved in Campania in Italy and by the Greeks in Sunion . . . it grows in wild and wooded places, and that garlands have been made from it from old time is shown in the name *sertula* which it hath taken. In fragrance it is like the saffron crocus, itself being white."

For discussion of the *Copa* see Robinson Ellis, *Appendix Vergiliana*, 1912; his article, *Further Notes on the Ciris, etc.*, in the *American Journal of Philology*, viii. 1887, pp. 399–414; Bembo's letter to Strozzi, *Ad Herculem Strottium de Virgilii Culice*, Venice, 1530; on Mico, Traube in *Poetae Latini Carolini Aevi*, iii. pp. 271 ff.; Ellis, *Journal of Philology*, xxii. pp. 9–21; on Angilbert, see Hariulfus, *Cronica Centulensis*, lib. ii.; Dümmler in *P.L.C.*, I. pp. 355 ff.; on

serta, Cato, *De Agri Cultura,* 107, 113; Pliny, *Nat. Hist.*
xxi. 9, 29.

PETRONIUS ARBITER   P. 6

d. c. A.D. 66

"Most men toil for it," said Tacitus, "but this man
loitered into fame. Not that he was ever accounted the
glutton or the profligate; the scholar, rather, the artist, of
exquisite living." Nero lumbered after him, heavy footed
and earnest, Caliban after Ariel. Petronius was his
Arbiter of Elegance: nothing could be agreeable till it
had passed the bar of that fastidious judgment. Thanks
to that same discrimination, he had been a vigorous
administrator in the provinces, where his part demanded
it: once in Rome, the old mask fitted easily, and steadily
day by day, the material for his great novel grew, the dis-
gusts, the will o' the wisp of flickering passion, the mon-
strous unshared comedy of things. But his own particular
monster was ceasing to be a good monster; the Emperor's
sudden displeasure gave him his cue. He died by his own
hand, very leisurely, with time to converse not indeed of
the immortality of the soul, as was fashionable on such
occasions, but of idle verses; remembering too to smash
the myrrhine bowl that Caliban had always coveted. This
might not be death in the high Roman fashion, and Tacitus
felt it; but he is as much a victim as Caliban, or that shy
scholar John of Salisbury ten centuries away, to this strange
un-Roman charm.

They were very like the eighteen-nineties, this crowd
who exclaimed in ecstasy over a dying mullet, pointing
out to one another the fading crimsons of its little labouring
belly: and Petronius among them is not unlike their elfin

caricaturist. There was a grace of casualness about him, said Tacitus, a sort of unconcern, that gave him a curious *simplicitas*. Tacitus, beyond all historians, has the humanity that means the gift of divination; he had pierced to the secret spring, the spirit that corruption could not touch, the Petronius not of the *Satyricon*, but of the thirty-odd poems scattered through mediæval anthologies. It is true that they are of uncertain ascription in the manuscript, and at any rate mediæval ascription goes for little, but whoever wrote the fragments in the novel,

" Ah God, ah God, that night when we two lay "
(*Qualis nox fuit illa, di deaeque,*)

and the lament for the desolate waters where the wild birds float no more (*Iam Phasidos unda*), wrote also the

Sit nox illa diu nobis dilecta, Nealce,

and the

O litus vita mihi dulcius, O mare !

Tradition has him born near Marseilles, the first Provençal poet, countryman to Bernart de Ventadorn rather than to Horace; and it was there, three centuries later, that Sidonius Apollinaris saw him a familiar ghost, at home among the immemorial olive trees as " that other little godship, for whom the countryman still lights his twinkling lamp." He died about A.D. 66: two years later, in 68, Nero too was dead, in the thirty-first year of his age.

Texts in Baehrens, *Poetae Latini Minores*, iv. 81, 84, 99, 100, 101, 94, 121. *Qualis nox* is from the *Satyricon*, ed. Buecheler, 1912, p. 55. See also Tacitus, *Annal.* xvi. 18, 19; Pliny, *Nat. Hist.* xxxvii. 2, 7; Sidonius Apollinaris, *Carmina*, xxiii. 155–7.

PULCHRA COMIS P. 20

(*Young and gold-haired*)

THE quatrain comes from a ninth-century MS. in the British Museum (Royal MS. 15. B. xix), parts of which certainly belonged to the library of St. Rémy at Rheims, as is stated in the note that curses anyone stealing it. It includes some writings of Bede, the satires of Persius, an A.B.C. on the voices of animals (bees *abizant*, elephants *brariant*), and farewell verses from the Irishman Colman to another Colman, about to start for home (see p. 74). The ninth-century scribe attributes the *Pulchra comis* to Virgil, but Aldhelm of Sherborne who knew it also thought that Ovid wrote it, and quoted it as an example of the amphimacric foot, *ut Ovidius ' dulce quiescenti basia blanda dabas.'*

See B.M. Royal MS. 15 B. xix. fº 99ᵇ. *Anthologia Latina*, 674; Aldhelm, *De Metris*, cxxii.

TE VIGILANS OCULIS: P. 22
O BLANDOS OCULOS

(*By day mine eyes: O lovely restless eyes*)

THESE two lyrics are from a strange anthology that was compiled in the late ninth or early tenth century, and took cover behind the vast respectable bulk of the *Etymology* of Isidore of Seville. The manuscript, now lost, belonged to the cathedral library of St. Sylvius at Beauvais, which was wrecked in the Revolution. Some of its MSS. made their way to the Bibliothèque Nationale, but no trace of the *Codex Isidori Bellovacensis* has been found. It is the only source for some of the loveliest lyrics of the Latin Anthology, among them eleven or twelve by Petronius, and the untranslatable splendour of the *Amare liceat si potiri non licet*,

" Still let me love though I may not possess." [1]

That they survive at all is due to the labour of Claude Binet, biographer of Ronsard, who transcribed the poems and published them at Poitiers in 1579, with the characteristic Renaissance motto in Latin and French, *Vitam mortuo reddo, Je r'avie le mort*. In the twelfth century, Beauvais had been a great school of the humanities. Radulfus of Beauvais, who had been Abelard's pupil, taught there, and it was to him that Peter of Blois wrote, upbraiding him for his indecorous enthusiasm for antiquity: " Priscian and Tully, Lucan and Persius: these be thy gods." Helinand, the scholar-trouvère who afterwards turned monk, studied there, in the days when the whole world seemed too narrow for a temperament as restless as a flying bird: and its fame lingers in the name of Vincent of Beauvais, the last of the humanists before darkness fell upon the universities in the fourteenth century. There are already shadows on the good Vincent: it was he who said that Petronius Arbiter was a holy bishop of Bologna, who died under Diocletian and wrote Lives of the Desert Fathers, and evidently the legend persisted, for Claude Binet refutes it with some asperity in his preface.

See the *Anthologia Latina*, 702, 714; Claude Binet: *C. Petroni. Arbitri itemque aliorum veterum epigrammata hactenus non edita, Cl. Binetus conquisivit et nunc primum publicavit*. Poitiers, 1579.) Peter of Blois, *Epist.* vi. (Migne, 207, c. 18); Helinand, *Epistola ad Galterum* (Migne, 212, c. 748).

[1] Translation by George Saintsbury.

DIC QUID AGIS   P. 24

(Lovely Venus, what's to do ?)

Dic quid agis is from the great seventh or eighth century *Codex Salmasianus*, written in uncials, and now in Paris. It once belonged to Claude de Saumaise, the Salmasius who was Milton's rival, and rebuked him for his unbridled and amatorious reading. There is no knowledge as to where it was written and what were its haunts before the seventeenth century. The first reference to it is by Salmasius himself, " an ancient book, which I was made a present of by the learned and ingenious Jean Lacurne, of judgment singularly chaste, whom I mention for his honouring." Jean Lacurne was baillie of Arnay-le-Duc, not a great way from Cluny, whose magnificent library of 1,800 MSS. was scattered and spoiled in the Wars of Religion, and it has been suggested that it may have been yet another of the treasures of Cluny, and have passed into the hands of a neighbouring book-lover; but there is no mention of it in the twelfth-century catalogue. Riese, who edited it for the *Anthologia Latina*, believes it a copy of an anthology made in Africa during the sixth century, probably by the African poet Luxorius, or by a friend, since his own indifferent poetry bulks largely in it. There are quotations from Virgil, Ovid, Propertius, but for the most part from poets of the fifth and sixth century: a lyric *Aurea mala* by Petronius, and above all the *Pervigilium Veneris*.

See *Anthologia Latina*, pp. xii–xxiii, 24; Gaston Boissier, *Revue Critique*, 1869, pp. 198–201.

AUSONIUS AND PAULINUS
OF NOLA

c. 310–c. 395   353–431

A GOOD deal of the poetry of Ausonius belongs to his old age in Bordeaux, a vintage as mellow as the claret that still keeps his name " in pleasantness and blessing," as John of Salisbury said of two good scholars dead. He was over seventy when he wrote his Memoirs, with little but pleasantness to put on record, and barely enmity enough to serve as grindstone to an epigram. The death of his young wife was his one sharp sorrow; she died when she was still " the little lass " that he had thought to find her even in her old age. Writing thirty-six years after it, the house is still empty about him: but her children lived, and the boy had come to high offices of State. It is the things which Ausonius reveals unconsciously that win him liking, not those which he sets out to celebrate with a kind of innocent pomp: not the chair of rhetoric at twenty-five, nor the imperial tutorship in his fifties, nor the consulship at sixty-nine, but that he loved and taught rhetoric all his life, and kept his simplicity: that he was a scholar without jealousy: that the boy he taught so loved him that when he became emperor nothing was too good for his old tutor, till finally he has him sitting, bewildered and happy, in the ivory chair. Gratian was assassinated in 383, and even in this Ausonius was fortunate, for it meant release from offices the old grammarian was hardly fit for, and a return to his " walled garden with its quiet paths," *nidus senectutis*, he called it, the nest of his old age.

There is a good deal of correspondence from the villa at Bordeaux, steeped in the vast leisure of the ancient world. To Theon, commending the flavour and lamenting the fewness of his oysters: to Theon, complaining of the badness of his poems over against the goodness of his apples; who would think they were chips of the same block? to Symmachus, verses, after a night of wine and flutes—" but do you read them also a little flown and *dilutior*; for it is outrageous that a strictly abstemious reader should sit in judgment upon a poet a little drunk." There is no quarrelling with life, no suggestion of the questioning that sometimes breaks through the equally mannered letters of Sidonius Apollinaris a century later, once in a cry far beyond anything he ever wrote in verse: " O abject necessity of being born: O hard necessity of living: O sharp necessity of dying!" Yet we may call no man happy this side death: it was the last decade of Ausonius' life that broke his heart.

" And so, Paulinus, you cast off the yoke— "

to the reader of the letters in the casual ordering of the older editions, the opening sentence comes like thunder out of a blue sky. Gradually the story pieces itself together. Paulinus, governor of a province and consul before he was thirty, was the pupil of whom a Roman master dreamed: Ausonius is never weary of recalling that in the consulship the pupil had preceded his master. Now with political honours behind him, he had come to settle down on the Aquitaine estate, and follow the laurel of Apollo which no less surely awaited him. One notes that Rome is no longer the goal of poets, and the Midi with its tradition of Greek culture will be the nucleus of light for centuries. It was to Desiderius at Vienne that the Blessed Gregory wrote in wrath and grief, for that he sang the songs of Apollo, and the grammarians of Toulouse argue over the vocative of *ego* amid the crash of empires. There are four letters to Paulinus, casual and gay, thanks for a new savoury, a harassed bailiff, an exchange of verses, affectionate chiding of the younger man's reluctance to create.

Then, suddenly, emptiness and silence. Paulinus had taken a sudden journey into Spain, presumably on some business connected with his wife's estates, but no man certainly knew the reason. He gave no explanation, took leave of no one, not even so much as the *salve* of courteous enemies for which Ausonius pleaded. No message came from him. Lover and friend he had put far from him, and his acquaintance into darkness. There followed four years of impenetrable and cruel silence.

Four years is a long time at seventy, and Ausonius loved him. Letter follows letter, of affectionate raillery—a pox upon this Spain!—of passionate appeal that checked itself for lack of dignity and still broke out afresh, of bitter and wounding reproach. Yet it seems not wholly to have been Paulinus' fault, unless that he had deliberately gone into retreat so strait that no rumour from his old world could reach him. At the end of the four years three letters came to him by a single messenger, and he hastens to make what amends he could. At best, it is written from a great way off. "As a dream when one awaketh, so shalt thou despise their image." Apollo, the Muses, the dusty laurels, what were these to the man

"Whom Joy hath overtaken as a flood,"

whom "long eternity" has greeted with its "individual kiss"? The small tuneful business of the old days is too clearly the dance of gnats above a stream in summer. Ausonius had not spared him; there is a trace of Rutilius Namatianus' bitterness against this new Circe of a religion that made men's minds brutal, not their bodies; but Paulinus has no resentment. He has chosen. Henceforth his mind is a torch, flaming through the secrets of eternity. But his heart aches for his old master, and the gratitude, all but adoration, he lavishes upon him might have deceived most men. It did not deceive Ausonius. The letter in

which he makes answer is poignant enough; but the super-
scription is more poignant still—" To Paulinus, when he
had answered other things, but had not said that he would
come." Eternity? He words me, he words me. One
thing was clear to Ausonius:

> " Nous n'irons plus au bois,
>   Les lauriers sont coupés."

And this time he gives up argument, speaks no longer of a
lost career, of great promise starved, but pleads for love's
sake only.

> " And so, Paulinus, you cast off the yoke—"

There follow pages that have only one parallel, the cry
from Po Chu-i in exile, four centuries later—" O Wei-chih,
Wei-chih! This night, this heart. Do you know them or
not? Lo Tien bows his head." Then Ausonius falls to
dreaming; he hears the grating of the boat on the beach,
the shouting of the people in the street, the footsteps, the
familiar knock on the door.

> " Is't true? or only true that those who love
>   Make for themselves their dreams? "

That wounding spearhead of Virgil reached its mark.
Paulinus answered in something like an agony of love and
compassion. Once again he pleaded the mystery that no
man sees from without: then the crying of his own heart
silenced the sober elegiacs, and he breaks into one of the
loveliest lyric measures of the ancient world.

> " I through all chances that are given to mortals—"

After this there is silence. Whether Ausonius laid it to his
heart, or wrote again above it, " But did not say that he
would come," there is no showing. A few years saw him
go down to his grave, a shock of corn fully ripe, full of

years and honour, his children and grandchildren to mourn him: the same years saw Paulinus parish priest of the shrine of St. Felix at Nola.

> " To guard thy altar through the silent night,
> And sweep thy floor and keep thy door by day,
> And watch thy candles burn—"

" *voilà le rêve de ce sénateur et de ce consulaire.*" Year after year his devotion to his saint brings an ode for his feast, the 14th of January, cheerful and sweet, like a robin singing in the snows: the loveliest written for that eternal April of the heart which was to flower in the twelfth century, the faint clear colouring of the first spring flowers, crocus and almond blossom. But never again is he the lark singing at heaven's gate: never again so stung by the *lacrimae rerum*, the blindness and the pain of solitary hearts, the suffering divinity of human passion, as to transmute its anguish into ecstasy.

" The poetical fame of Ausonius," said Gibbon in an acid footnote, " condemns the taste of his age." A good deal of it is sad stuff: the elegant trifles that weigh like lead on later generations. But his *De Rosis Nascentibus*, in its own phrase, " lives again in each succeeding rose." Despériers of Lyons translated it, after twelve hundred years,

> " Un jour de mai que l'aube—"

and Ronsard caught the echo of it from him,

> " Mignonne, allons voir si la rose—"

and after him Spenser in a slower melody,

> " Gather the rose of love, whilest yet is time,"

and after him the Cavalier lyrists in the loveliest melody of all. *Cupido Cruciatus* is the new romantic imagination working on Virgil, himself romatic enough, and in the fields of the Sorrowful Lovers, from a phrase or two in his original,

> *" per incertam lunam sub luce maligna*
> *Est iter in silvis,"*

he has created the twilight world of Western Europe.   As for the *Mosella*, it is a mirror of quiet observation.   Edward Fitzgerald was so haunted by the lovely pause after the *tremit absens*, that he scribbled a fragment, adapted from Shelley, to his friend Cowell

> "—in Time's fleeting river
> The image of that little vine-leaf lay,
> Immovably unquiet—and for ever
> It trembles—but it cannot pass away."

The text used for the poems of Ausonius is the edition by Schenkl (*Mon. Germ. Hist.*, 1883).   *De Rosis Nascentibus*, p. 243; *Mosella*, ll. 192–195, p. 88; *Silva Myrtea* from *Cupido Cruciatus*, ll. 5–9, p. 121 ; *Ad Uxorem*, Epigr. xviii, p. 200.

For Paulinus of Nola, the edition by Hartel (*Corpus Script. Eccles. Lat.*, xxx., Vienna, 1894). *Non inopes animi* from Carmen x. ll. 162–180. *Ego te per omne*, Carmen xi. ll. 49–68. *Ver avibus*, Carmen xxiii. ll. 1–20. *Cerne deum*, Carmen xxvii. ll. 284–306.

PRUDENTIUS   P. 42

348–c. 405

NOTHING is known of Aurelius Prudentius Clemens, the greatest and least egotistical of the Christian Latin poets, except the little that he himself tells us ; that he was born when " old Salias " was consul, and that when he came to write the preface to his Book of Hours, the snows were upon his head. He writes of three towns of Northern Spain, Tarragona, Calahorra, Saragossa, as *nostras urbes*, but with especial intimacy of the last: and of " the folk of the Pyrenees " as his own people. His life was spent in the law-courts: he rose to high judicial office under the Emperor Theodosius, like himself a plain Spanish gentle-man; and when he was fifty-seven, turned from these things to find the kingdom of God. Looking back upon his life he remembers as Augustine did the sins of his youth, but also

> " How many times the rose
> Returnèd after snows."

He does not speak of any formal vows: his communion is the communion of those forgotten saints, before whose unnumbered ashes he had knelt in Rome, and for whom he made his *Peristephanon* of grave remembrance. Augustine, Jerome, and Ambrose were his contemporaries, and have left a greater name: even Fortunatus has been sainted, but not Prudentius. Yet his phrases are the naked poetry of religion: and in an age when goodness might easily have become a negative virtue of denial and renunciation, he proved, like Donne, that learning could be " Christ's ambassador," and " Beauty, paradise's flower." To trans-late him is impossible: and if these halting versions have been included, it is because any collection of mediæval lyric is poor unless his shadow falls across it.

The texts are taken from the edition by J. Bergman, *Corpus Scriptorum Ecclesiasticorum Latinorum*, lxi. (Vienna, 1926), *Hymnus ante somnum*, p. 32, ll. 9–20, 149–153; *Hymnus circa Exsequias Defuncti*, p. 56, ll. 125–end. For the auto-biographical references in his poems see the Prolegomena.

BOETHIUS P. 48

c. 480–524

IN 524, Anicius Manlius Severinus Boethius, ex-consul and Roman senator, died by order of Theodoric under torture in the dungeon of Pavia in his forty-fifth year. He had been Theodoric's most trusted counsellor; Theodoric had looked up to him with the admiration of the great barbarians for the Romans who were politically their servants and spiritually their lords. But the Gothic king grew old and wary and suspicious; Boethius for his part had too much the intransigeance of the Platonist turned politician. Intransigeance can look like treason, and in a sudden outburst of savagery, Theodoric had him done to death. Two years later, he himself was dead, Procopius said of remorse, under the pitiful great bulk of his tomb at Ravenna: the other had already entered on his immortality. His work as interpreter of Greek to Roman thought, in mathematics, in music, above all the translation and comment on Aristotle, would have kept his fame alight among the scholars: but the *Consolation of Philosophy* written in prison, in presence of torture and imminence of death, has made his name as gracious as a benediction.

The texts are from the Teubner edition of the *De Philosophiae Consolatione : Quaenam discors*, Book V. 3; *Stupet tergeminus*, iii. 12, ll. 29–58; *Si vis celsi iura*, iv. 6, ll. 1–18; *Ite nunc fortes*, iv. 7, ll. 32–5. In the Eurydice poem it has been pointed out that unless Orpheus is pronounced in the Elizabethan manner, which offends the classical ear, the line

Orpheus saw Eurydice

halts by a half-foot, and that the monosyllable *saw* should be replaced by some longer verb. Yet Orpheus is so heavy

296

a dissyllable that any variant seems to me to crowd the line, like hurrying a tolling bell.

VENANTIUS FORTUNATUS   P. 58

c. 530–c. 603

Venantius Fortunatus, "who is so charming," says Professor Saintsbury, " that they ought to have called him A-venantius," is a kind of halcyon on the dangerous Frankish seas. He was born at Trieste, and though he was afterwards to know the wildness of the Breton coast, the Adriatic was the horizon of his youth. His learning, as gay and perhaps as shallow as mosaic, he got in Ravenna; sometime in his thirties he set out from it to give St. Martin thanks for restoring the eyesight he had lost there, and came dallying through France on his way to the sovereign shrine of the Saint at Tours, visiting bishops and great ones, and leaving behind him a trail of little verses. The record of the journey is in the eleven books of poems which he collected in his old age at the convenient request of his friend Gregory, Bishop of Tours, who admired a talent so much more decorative than his own historian's prose: they are little letters in verse, reminiscences of dinners where the fish was as subtly flavoured as the Falernian, of churches where the sunlight wavered on the ceiling as on sea-water, of the midday halt in a wood, July heat and dust and the lapse of spring water and a tired man lying on the grass and chanting Virgil to himself, or the Psalms. He was for a while at court, writing an epithalamion for Sigebert and Brunhild, and poems on the queen's apple-orchard: the grandsons of Chlovis, the great barbarian who first wore the Roman purple, were ruling and quartering France among them, with bursts of astonishing savagery, but no wind blew rough against Fortunatus. All men liked him, and he had the sensitive kind of friendship that could forbear leave-taking because his friend was tired and still asleep. Finally, in 567, his wanderings brought him to Poitiers, to the abbey which Radegunde had founded, and which her living presence had already made a shrine.

It was then thirty-six years since Clothair had brought her from the sack of her uncle's house in a punitive expedition against Thuringia, to grow up into his reluctant queen: but the grave charm that had looked out at him from the eyes of a child, and that kept him for twenty years bewitched and at bay, was about her still. Some divinity hedged her: his last wild pursuit of her ended in penitence as for sacrilege before St. Martin's altar, and the gift of the abbey lands in perpetual possession. There she lived, cruel to herself but gentle to all men, and compassionate above all to poor captives, with the memory of her own childish anguish still quick in the poem that Fortunatus made from her telling of it. Her influence fell on him like a consecration. Sensitive to all beauty, of the spirit or the flesh, and capable of strange and high exaltations, he settled down beside her, took holy orders, and in his old age was consecrated Bishop of Poitiers in the church where his body was laid. Two hundred years later Paul the Deacon, another Italian poet and exile, came to his grave and wrote his epitaph.

Criticism has been hard on Fortunatus. " *Le poète épicuréen, l'abbé gastronome,*" says Ampère, a little unkindly, and undoubtedly a good deal of his life did consist in eating and drinking. Radegunde indulged him, with the tolerance that sometimes accompanies great personal austerity. Fortunatus writes little verses about a tablecloth of roses and ivy, thanks for eggs and plums: he is to eat two eggs a day, and he has eaten four: may all the days of his life

obey her as did his greed this day. But there was no gross-
ness in him, and there were times when fire was laid upon
his lips. *Vexilla regis prodeunt* was written for the coming
of a fragment of the Holy Rood to Poitiers: five hundred
years later it was the marching song of the men who
fought for the Sepulchre. If he loved good cheer, he loved
goodness more: and he had as absolute a vision as that
older materialist and mystic of the ladder between earth
and heaven.

The text of the poems is from the edition by F. Leo in
the *Monumenta Germaniae Historiae*, 1881.

Tempora si solito, Bk. VIII. 6. "*pariter habeatis utraque*"
includes Agnes, Radegunde's adopted daughter and abbess
of the convent, to whom Fortunatus wrote some of his
prettiest verses.

O regina potens, VIII. 8. It was Radegunde's custom in
Lent to go into utter solitude.

Altaris domini pollens, III. 26: written from an island off
the coast of Brittany to his friend Rucco in Paris.

Nectar vina cibus, VII. 2: written to Gogo, a great
Frankish noble. The Apicius of the text was the author of
ten books on cookery, who finally committed suicide,
finding life intolerable on an income reduced to ten million
sesterces a year.

Tempora lapsa volant, VII. 12. A fragment of elegiacs
written to Iovinus, governor of Provence. *Naso* is an
emendation for the *Lysa* of the text.

For the life, see Paul the Deacon, *Historia Langobardorum*,
ii. 13. *Vita S. Radegundis*, begun by Fortunatus. (*M.G.H.
Script. Rer. Mer.* ii. 358 ff.)

521–597

ST. COLUMBA was born at Gartan in Donegal on December 7th, 521, and died before the altar in the monastery chapel on Iona a little after midnight on the 5th of June, 597. The tradition that he wrote the *Altus Prosatur*, of which this stanza is a fragment, is an old one, and its rhythms accord well enough with the great voice that sent the strophes of the XLIVth Psalm striding the hills like thunder peals and volleying against the walls of the Pictish dun. According to one of the curious Irish-Latin prefaces, the *Altus Prosator* was seven years in writing, in a dark cell without light, in atonement for the great fight with Diarmuid the High-king at Cooldrevne, in which Columba had remembered rather that he was great-great-grandson of Niall of the Nine Hostages than that he was a man of God. Another says that it was " suddenly made," on a day when Colum Cille was in Iona, and nobody was with him but Baithinn, and they had no food except a sieve of oats. And Colum Cille said to Baithinn, " Nobler guests are coming to us to-day, O Baithinn," which were folk of Gregory coming with presents to him.   And he asked what food there was, and when he heard he bade Baithinn stay and look to the guests, while himself went to the mill.   So he took the sack of oats from the stone that is in the refectory at Iona, and put it on his shoulders, but his burden felt heavy to him, so he composed the hymn *Adiutor laborantium* from there up to the mill.   Now when he put the first handful into the mill, he began the first capitulum of the *Altus*, " and the composition of the hymn and the grinding of the corn were completed together, nor was it as the fruit of meditation, but by the grace of God."

Now Gregory's folk had brought rich presents, the Cross

which is called the Great Gem, and the Hymns of the Week, and in return Colum Cille gave them the hymn to take back to Gregory. But as they went eastward they made three stanzas of their own in place of those Colum Cille had written. And when they began to read it to Gregory God's angels came and stood listening, and Gregory too stood up. But when the false verses were reached the angels of God sat down, and Gregory sat down also. So the messengers confessed and got forgiveness: and Gregory said the hymn would be the best of all praises if Colum Cille had not too slightly commended the Trinity *per se*, as well as in Its creatures: and when Colum Cille heard this he composed the *In te, Christe*.

This stanza is the first use in poetry of the tremendous rhythms of the Vulgate version of Zephaniah: *Juxta est dies Domini magnus, juxta est et velox nimis : vox diei Domini amara, tribulabitur ibi fortis. Dies irae dies illa, dies tribulationis et angustiae, dies calamitatis et miseriae, dies tenebrarum et caliginis, dies nebulae et turbinis, dies tubae et clangoris super civitates munitas et super angulos excelsos.* It is the indestructible radium that transfigures the *De Fide Catholica* of Hrabanus Maurus in the ninth ventury, the *Prose of the Dead* of St. Martial of Limoges in the tenth, till finally in the *Dies Irae* of Thomas of Celano it burns through the inmost veil of heaven. But the human sadness of the last lines, on the ending of the love of women and of desire, is neither in the Vulgate, nor in the *Dies Irae*.

"There are many graces upon this hymn," says the Irish commentator, "namely, angels present during its recitation: no demon shall know the path of him who shall recite it every day, and foes shall not put him to shame on the day he shall recite it; and there shall be no strife in the house where its recitation shall be customary: aye, and it protects against every death except death on the pillow, neither shall there be famine nor nakedness in the place where it shall be oft recited: and there are many others."

The text and prefaces, here abridged, are in the *Irish Liber Hymnorum*, i. 66 ff., ii. pp. 23–27, Bernard and Atkinson (Henry Bradshaw Society, 1898): for the life of Columba see Adamnan, *Vita S. Columbae*; the story of the singing of the CXLIVth Psalm is in Book I. chapter 37.

A SCHOLAR OF MALMESBURY   P. 70

Eighth Century

AT the end of the famous ninth-century Vienna MS. of the letters of St. Boniface, the apostle of Germany, are five poems for a long time attributed to Aldhelm, abbot of Malmesbury in 675, and Bishop of Sherborne, 705–709, whose memory Alfred held in great reverence. It is Alfred who told the story of how the bishop used to stand as a gleeman on the bridge, singing fragments of the Gospel interspersed with scraps of clowning, if by any means he could win men's ears and then their souls. For a long time it was thought that these poems might be his, the very *opuscula* for which Lull wrote to Dealwin, asking him to send them out to him, " for the consoling of my pilgrimage and in memory of that blessed bishop." Yet this poem is evidently addressed to him, not written by him, for there is a pun on Aldhelm, the " old helmet," in the opening line,

" Lector cassis catholica,"

and it is more probably written by one of his clerks, sent on some errand through Devon and Cornwall, then part of the diocese of Sherborne. It is the story of a miraculous escape, the crash of the abbey buildings in a furious storm, the abbey church in which the brethren were singing matins alone left standing. That the writer was a scholar of Malmesbury seems probable from the Irish character of the metre, and the wild clamour of strange and barbaric words. Aldhelm himself had it from Maildulf who founded Malmesbury, and the schools of Hadrian and Theodore at Canterbury never quite rid him of his passion for splendid and far-fetched speech.

For text and discussion of authorship see Ehwald, *Aldhelmi opera* (1909), pp. 519 *et seq.*: Henry Bradley in the *English Historical Review*, 1900, p. 291.

COLMAN THE IRISHMAN P. 74

ALL that is certainly known of these verses is that they were written by an old Irishman, Colman, to a younger of the same name, on the eve of his journey back to Ireland. They are in the same ninth-century MS. compiled at Rheims (now in the British Museum) as the *Pulchra comis*. Wilhelm Meyer first transcribed them in 1906 and sent the copy to Kuno Meyer, who published it with further emendations in *Eriù*, 1907.

The name Colman, Little Dove, is one of the commonest in the early Irish church, probably because of the great fame of St. Columba. The Martyrology of Donegal mentions 113, says Kuno Meyer, one a Colman from Fahan with the nickname *imrama* (" of the Voyage ") whose day is July 8th, another *ailithir* (the pilgrim) from Inis Mochol Móc, for November 7th. The B.M. catalogue suggests Colman, Bishop of Lindisfarne 661–668, who came back to Ireland and founded a monastery at Inishboffin, with thirty men of English race and many Irishmen who had come back with him. But there was no peace among them, says Bede, for when the summer and the time of harvest came the Irish took a desire of wandering, and then with the cold returned home to eat those things which their brethren had laboured in harvesting. And the contention was so strong that Colman built a new monastery for the English on the mainland, and no more is said of the improvident grasshoppers (*Hist. Eccles.* iv. 4).

Kuno Meyer inclines to the ninth century and a continental source, from the date and provenance of the MS.: there were many Irishmen in Northern France in the beginning of the ninth century. He also suggests that *nubiferi auri* (l. 32) should be *nubiferi euri*, in memory of Silius Italicus, x. 322, the south-east wind which would carry the pilgrim from France to south-west England, or for that matter to Cork itself.

The text is from MS. Royal 15 B xix. f° 69, with emendations gratefully acknowledged to Kuno Meyer, *Eriù*, 1907, pp. 186–9.

The *vates* (l. 14) is of course Virgil, and the lines are a mosaic of Bucolics ix. 51, Aen. v. 395, vii. 440.

ALCUIN   P. 78

c. 735–804

In 804, Alcuin, a Yorkshireman, died in his abbey of St. Martin at Tours in his seventieth year. In the spring of 801, three years before his death, he had written to his old friend the Archbishop of York, with a little present of wine, *for you and the brethren and our friends*—Alcuin had the humanist's palate for wine and an un-English dislike of beer—and an entreaty that the Archbishop will not let his reading rust, *lest all my labour in collecting books be lost.* The Cathedral Library at York (the same which Bede must have used) had been Alcuin's passion; he was librarian and Master of the Schools there until Charlemagne, great strategist that he was, persuaded him to Aachen, to put an empire and an emperor to school. For ten years he taught there, and at last, in 796, craved leave to retire to his abbey in Touraine. There he still taught, not only as to his scholar Daphnis the spiritual significance of the 600 wives and 900 concubines of Solomon, but Latin verses. His loveliest lyric, the Cuckoo, is a lament for a vanished scholar, "so late begotten, and so quickly lost," who had fallen into evil ways. He had two defections to grieve him. One, Osulf, never came back, and the story goes that Alcuin cried after him in grief, ' *He shall die neither in this nor yet in his own land.' Which the issue afterwards proved, for he died in Lombardy.* The other, and more like to be the subject of his poem, did come back. He was with him in that April of 801, and his messenger to York, still his *avis vernalis. The aforesaid fowl*—Alcuin's humour is always charming and academic and absurd—*will tell you of my infirmity, but glory be to God I am something better*, though *the old integrity of body hath not yet returned. Pray for me : for the time draws nigh that this hostel must be left behind and I go out to things unknown."* A little later, " *As I said to the Cuckoo, I have laid aside the pastoral care, and now sit quietly at St. Martin's, waiting for the knocking at the gate."* Not many could rise up to answer it with a more confident heart, but his epitaph has the wistful diffidence of all good men. The lament for his empty cell is among his poems and in his own manner, but more likely from the hand of his disciple Fredugis.

The *Conflictus Veris et Hiemis* has been taken from him, because the line " The goats come to the milking, udders full," is reminiscent of Horace, and it is argued that Horace was unknown on the continent until the middle of the ninth century, when the Irishmen wrote the MS. now at Berne. Yet the Berne MS. must be a copy of a lost original : and even if that original was only known in Ireland, was in fact one of the books that St. Paul helped Coelchu of Clonmacnoise to carry on the road, it is to be remembered that Alcuin called Coelchu " magister," and wrote him letters of affectionate gossip, and that he was devoted, for other reasons besides a similar palate for wine, to Joseph the Scot. And also that the line, however reminiscent of Horace (which was Alcuin's self-chosen nickname) is not beyond the range of any countryman's imagination.

Text: Dümmler, *Poet. Lat. Car.* 1.

Heu, cuculus, Carmina 57; *Conflictus Veris et Hiemis,* 58; *De Luscinia,* 61; *De Sancto Michaelo,* 120; *Epitaphium,* 123. *O mea cella* (Fredugis), 23. See also *Alcuini Epistolae,* 226, 233: Paul von Winterfeld, *Rhein. Mus.* 1905, pp. 31 ff.

MS. OF MONTE CASSINO   P. 100

Greeting from Charlemagne's court, written before 795

IN the library at Monte Cassino there is a manuscript written by Peter the Deacon who was librarian there in the early years of the twelfth century. It includes a few anonymous poems, written in another hand, but corrected by Peter; and among them is this greeting to the brethren at Monte Cassino, with affectionate messages to Paul the Deacon, who was a brother there. The tradition in the monastery in the twelfth century was that the writer was Charlemagne himself: and Leo of Ostia in his *Cronica* has a long story of the intimacy between emperor and scholar, and how Charlemagne in his anger at finding his scholar still loyal to his first master, the Desiderius whom Charlemagne had deposed from the throne of Lombardy, was for blinding him, and rued, saying, " But where shall I find such another poet? " and exiled him to an island from which Paul after some years escaped, first to Beneventum where the daughter of his old master was Duchess, and then to Monte Cassino, where he wrote his *History of the Lombards*, and died in peace: and where Charlemagne deigned to write him verses as affectionate as these.

It is a good story, with a flavour of the Arabian Nights about it; but contemporary documents are silent on it. Paul called the Deacon came of a noble house of Friuli, and was much about the court, both at Pavia and at Beneventum, wrote poems to the Duchess there, and verses on Lake Como, on the scent of its myrtles and its ever-lasting spring. But Desiderius, king of Lombardy, was an orgulous prince, and a bad neighbour to the Roman See: Hadrian appealed to Charlemagne: the Frankish army crossed the Alps and invested Pavia: it fell in 774. Paul the Deacon became a monk at Monte Cassino, if indeed he had not already gone there, though he once said the Muses would rather have rose-gardens than the cloister. His brother went into captivity in France, the family property was confiscated. There were four children and a mother: at the end of six years she was begging their bread, *tremente ore*, with quivering mouth, on the streets. Paul himself was penniless, and in his desperation he bethought him of a direct appeal to the lion.

It seems that he won his suit, but from a phrase in a later letter, it was at a price: Charlemagne, who had the collector's passion, seems to have struck a bargain with him, the attendance of so admirable a poet at his own court. He lived there for some years, not ungrateful, recognizing the amazing charm of the gentle giant who held him, but homesick for the *alma tecta* of the beloved Benedict, heart-sick for the cloister. " Tell me when you write how the harvest went, and which of the brethren passed out from you this year. Some one told me Nonnus was dead: if that be so, half my heart has gone with him." At last he won his release: wrote the *History of the Lombards*, which has made him famous, and died in Monte Cassino in the Ides of April of some year unknown, leaving a legend of consummate scholarship and great gentleness.

These are not the only verses attributed to Charlemagne, and if it seems odd that the emperor who toiled at his slate in the middle of the night should have been judged capable of Latin verse, it is to be remembered that his wits were less clumsy than his fingers, and that he was admittedly as fluent in Latin as in his own Frankish tongue. Whatever his own efforts, he took enormous delight in the verse-making of his courtiers, Paul, and Peter of Pisa, and Angilbert and Alcuin and Theodulf, and was a shrewd judge of the small boys' verses in the Palace School. The suggestion that the poem was written by Alcuin in Charlemagne's name has one piece of internal evidence, for the homesickness of the lines on the cloister is echoed in letter after letter written home to York.

Text in Dümmler, *Poetae Latini Carolini Aevi*, i. p. 69. See also Leo of Ostia, *Cronica Monasterii Casinensis*, i. 15. (*M.G.H. SS.* vii. p. 592). *Epistolae Carolini Aevi*, ii. pp. 506 ff. *Archiv.* xii. p. 502.

ANGILBERT   P. 102

Fl. 841

NOTHING is known of the writer of this amazing dirge for the dead beyond what is evident in the poem, that his name was Angilbert, that he fought for Lothair in the fratricidal feud between the three sons of Louis at Fontenoy in Puisaye, June 25th, 841, and that the memory of a little farm in France turned into a reeking horror haunted him as it has haunted other poets fighting not very far from Fontenoy, but with more than ten centuries between. The carnage seems to have been frightful: *satis horrendum,* says one chronicler, briefly but adequately. Even the most stolid contemporaries speak of it with a kind of shudder: Regino of Prum says that it weakened the old valour of France, and left it helpless against the Northmen, who already in that year had sacked Rouen. The tenor of the poem suggests that Lothair was the victor: Charles and Louis claimed it, and professed themselves aggrieved that the Emperor had failed to recognize the judgment of God. Peace was finally made in 843 at Verdun, and the dismemberment of Charlemagne's empire into three kingdoms with other than their natural boundaries began, Louis the German being given districts on either side the Rhine for the sake of the vineyards, and the Emperor that fatal strip along the Rhine valley where the dragon's teeth are sown.

Text in Dümmler, *Poet. Lat. Car.* ii. p. 137. The poem is found set to music, extremely sorrowful, in a tenth-century MS. of St. Martial of Limoges, now in Paris (B.N. MS. Lat. 1154). See the facsimile in Coussemaker, *Histoire de l'harmonie au moyen âge,* pl. i–iv.

It also exists in a late ninth-century MS. of Farfa, now at St. Gall, written by a ruder hand, probably before the Saracens swept down on the great monastery and made it their stronghold.

HRABANUS MAURUS   P. 106

776–856

THE Blessed Alcuin had a weakness for giving nicknames. Besides the famous circle at court, David and Homer and Pindar, he called his friend the Bishop of Arno his Venerable

Fowl: and when Hrabanus came to Tours from Fulda to study the humanities, he called him Maurus, after Benedict's beloved disciple. Hrabanus came back to serve his own monastery as *scholasticus* and later, in 822, as abbot: an omnivorous reader and a voluminous writer, a good deal worried by administration—" seeing that these young ones have enough to eat is a great hindrance to one's reading," said he ruefully, and when the crash of his Emperor's fortunes in 842 made him resign his abbacy, it was not without secret jubilation that he settled with his books into a cell on the mountain side near the church of St. Peter. Lothair agreed with him: " the country quiet of the hills," he said, " is better for the spirit than the jangling of men." He had seven years of it, to read the poets and Holy Writ and finish his vast *De Universo*: then the new ruler, Louis the German, always eager for the friendship of this obstinate and loyal scholar, persuaded him from his retreat to the archiepiscopal see of Mainz, the town where he was born. He was consecrated in 847, ruled mightily for nine years; in three successive synods dealt with the incorrigible heretic Gottschalk; and himself died in 856, the greatest archbishop since Boniface. " If God," said Lothair once, " gave my predecessors in empire Jerome and Augustine and Ambrose, he gave me Hrabanus."

The story of his lifelong struggle with Gottschalk—literally lifelong, for the boy had been brought as a mere child to the monastery by his knightly father, and grew up in wild rebellion—is too long to tell: it has the full cruelty of the struggle between two uncompromising idealists. Gottschalk was broken, in all but his spirit; yet from those broken strings came the most poignant lyric melody in Europe. Beside it, Hrabanus' verse is harsh and brazen: it is only now and then, as in the sudden confession to his old friend Grimold, abbot of St. Gall and perhaps the kindliest figure of his time, that one sees his human weakness and his self-distrust. His faith was absolute, self-condemning, and passionate: he saw the "sulphurous stagnant pools" of hell, the "incense-bearing fields of Paradise," and for sole hope of men, *Deus immensae bonitatis*, the huge kindliness of God. To faith such as this, heresy is more cruel than any purgatorial pain, and Gottschalk's heresy, the predestination of souls to damnation as well as to grace, was cruel enough. If Hrabanus could endure the sight of a man flogged into denying the truth as he saw it, and burning half-dead the book in which he had written it, he was fighting as best he knew the first menace of the Calvinism that was later to drive men insane. Moreover, it is difficult to think harshly of so great a lover of books: and when it came to his own prayers, the *Oratio Mauri ad Deum* is as wistful and despairing as Gottschalk's own.

Text in *Poet. Lat. Car.* ii. *Ad Grimoldum*, Carm. vi. *Ad Eigilum*, Carm. xxi. See also Migne, 107. 20, 26.

WALAFRID STRABO   P. 110

809–849

In the late summer of 849, Walafrid Strabo, abbot of Reichenau and certainly the ripest scholar of his years in Europe, came into France on an embassy to his old pupil, Charles the Bald. Meantime a young student of his went from Reichenau across the lake to St. Gall, while his master should be absent. The Abbot Grimold, who had fathered Walafrid in the quick promise of his youth, was very gracious with the boy who was Walafrid's pupil: Ermenric wrote afterwards how kindly they took him from the boat, and how gentle the brethren were. Two men especially he noted, whose spirits were lit candles, " and if the light of the one blazed the brighter, the other burnt more slowly and therefore the longer." He was still at St. Gall when the news was brought that the *maxima lux*, the light of his own abbey, had gone out;

> " Left thy beloved, thou that wert most beloved,
> O Walafrid, that art beneath this ground."

He died, " crossing the thirsty sands of the Loire," says one epitaph, and because ever since Orpheus came drifting

> " Down the swift Hebrus to the Lesbian shore,"

it has seemed a fitting end for poets, it is hazarded that he was drowned at the ford. They brought him back from the Loire valley to Reichenau, to " those low roofs " that had sheltered his poverty-stricken youth.

Walafrid's genius had flowered early. His *Visio Wettinis* was written in curious anticipation of Dante, from a story he had taken down himself from the lips of a dying brother at Reichenau: he was barely eighteen when he finished it, and dedicated it to Grimold. For Grimold, the great Frankish noble who was Louis' Chancellor and for thirty years Abbot of St. Gall, was one of those generous natures that are the enriching of many men's lives and leave small record of their own. His only monument is the library at St. Gall—they have still two leaves of his own Virgil there —and a few scattered references, dedications, letters in verse, from the men he befriended,

> ". . . anchor of weary ships
> Safe shore and land at last, thou, for my wreck."

It seems to have been his urgency that sent Walafrid to Fulda, where he was bitterly cold and woefully homesick, and where Hrabanus made him as massive a scholar as himself: nature had already made him a finer poet. But it was Grimold who had his heart, and when after some years at court as tutor to young Charles he came in 838, this time as abbot, to Reichenau, and made his garden there, it was to Grimold that he sent his book *Of Gardening*, and wrote what is perhaps the most famous dedication in mediæval Latin. The weight of Hrabanus' approval would lie heavy on the greater work, the *apparatus criticus* of Holy Writ that went into several editions even in the seventeenth century; but he would have been apt to trample on the *viridissima rutae silvula ceruleae*, the tiny sea-green forest of rue that spread in the shadow of the abbey trees. Yet it is Walafrid's *Hortulus* that still is green, while the volumes of the *Glossa Ordinaria* do but gather dust. "He was utterly simple," said Ermenric: and the tragedy of his early death is the myrrh that embalms his memory.

Hrabanus, now sixty-three and Archbishop of Mainz, composed the epitaph for the grave of his finest scholar. It is stiffly written, as was Hrabanus' wont, and intricate with reminiscences of the poets: it commends the faithful abbot, the admirable poet, the devout student of Holy Writ. Then at the last a sudden vivid memory of the dead man's charm came upon him, and where Fortunatus had written *noster et altus amor*, his heart wrote *almus*—

"Gentle, beloved, Death took you from us young."

The text of Walafrid's poems is edited by Dümmler in *Poet. Lat. Car.* ii. The sapphics on Reichenau (written surely not to Hrabanus, as Dümmler suggests, but to Grimold) are from *Carm.* 75: *De Cultura Hortorum, Carm.* 4 (27): *Ad Amicum, Carm.* 59. See also the *Epistola Ermenrici ad Grimoldum*, edited by Dümmler, 1873: the epitaph by Hrabanus, *P.L.C.* ii. p. 239: and an anonymous epitaph (from a MS. in the Bodleian), *ib.* p. 423.

SEDULIUS SCOTTUS   P. 118

Fl. 848–874

THERE is at Berne a Greek text of the Epistles of St. Paul with an interlinear Latin translation, believed to be in the actual handwriting of Sedulius: there is a commentary on the Psalms, also to his credit, and another on St. Jerome, with a political treatise *De Rectoribus Christianis*, written in admirable Latin: his friend the Irishman Cruindmelus acknowledged his collaboration in an *Art of Poetry*. Altogether, scholarship profound enough to ballast any craft; and undoubtedly Sedulius carried a good deal of sail.

Nothing is known of his earlier life in Ireland, or whether it was the dread of the Danes or simply what Walafrid Strabo once called " the Irish fashion of going away " that brought him to France. In 848, a mission came from Ireland to Charles the Bald, and Traube thinks that Sedulius may have been attached to it. However, it was less in the guise of ecclesiastical dignitaries than of *vagantes* that Sedulius and two of his friends arrived, tattered with wind and sodden with sleet, at the hospitable gates of the *évêché* at Liege. That Hartgar in entertaining them was entertaining " learned grammarians and pious priests," he had Sedulius' word: and he was scholar enough to recognize the first, and had perception enough to believe the second. Sedulius stayed on at Liége as *scholasticus* in the cathedral schools: wrote odes of welcome to visiting kings and emperors: had his verses embroidered by the empress Ermengard (she died in childbirth in 851, so that Sedulius must have been settled in Liége before that year):

wrote lovely lyrics for Christmas and for Easter, and
swinging *saturated songs* as he called them—

" Doth not the cork, redolent of balsam,
   Suffer the piercing of the iron corkscrew,
   Whence from the fissure floweth out a precious
      Drop of the liquor? "—

to Count Eberhard of Friuli and to Rodbert, to the depletion
of their cellars and the replenishing of his own. Count
Robert, " the golden hope of our Muse," gave him twenty-
five dozen once, and got in reply a lyric that still reads a
little drunk. That he continually grumbles is only to be
expected of a classical scholar, and of his nation, and to do
him justice he made his grumblings comical. He did not
like the east wind, nor leaks in his roof, nor draughts:
and, in this resembling the Emperor Julian in the same
region of the Meuse, he did not like the local beer, which
was, he said, a beast of prey in a philosopher's inwards.
But he was as hearty in his gratitude as in his grumbling,
and as sincere in his repentance as he was joyous in his
sinning. The monastery of Stavelot that kept the single
manuscript of his verse that has come down to us kept also
the Archpoet's: and their souls likewise are garnered in
one place.

   The text of the poems is edited by Traube in *Poet. Lat.
Car.* iii. The Easter poem, addressed to Tado, archbishop
of Milan, *Carmina* iii. 2. ll. 17–26: the intercession against
the plague, ii. 46: the complaint of thirst in spring, ii. 49:
his *apologia*, ii. 74. For his life, the best authority is in the
poems: but see also Traube, *Abhandlungen d. Kgl. Bayr.
Akad.* (Munich, 1891), pp. 339 ff.; Pirenne, *Mémoires
couronnés de l'Académie Royale de Belgique*, 1882; Hellmann,
Sedulius Scottus (Munich, 1906); Jarcho, *Die Vorläufer des
Golias*, in *Speculum*, 1928, pp. 523 ff

THE ABBOT OF ANGERS P. 126

Ninth Century

No language can be so gravely impish as mediæval Latin, and the clerks saw it early. One of the first exercises of their peculiar faculty is the *Cena Cypriani*, apparently based on St. Zeno's first communion addresses, in which, like many a great preacher since, he pictured the Holy Table stretching backwards into remote antiquity, with patriarchs and saints as *commensales*. *Cyprian's Feast* is a lively account of one such banquet, attended by most of the great ones from the Old and New Testaments, unfortunately recognizable by their less creditable peculiarities. It was not a wholly successful entertainment, inasmuch as Jonah proved a bad " mixer " (*male miscuerat*), Noah sat nodding, very drunk, Jacob was observed to be drinking out of his neighbour's glass as well as his own, John would drink nothing but water, and Tobit tried to leave early. Even the *pompa*, in which Adam came on as a gardener and Eve as a member of the ballet (*exodiana*), and Herod in character, was interrupted by the host's discovery that something had been stolen, and an inquisition out of which John the Baptist and St. Paul emerged with not unblemished characters, and Adam lost his job. All this, however, was a fine aid to memory, like the rhymes in the older Latin grammars: and Hrabanus himelf recommended it as such to Lothair II.

The *Cena Cypriani* was written by a certain John the Deacon: no one knows who wrote *The Abbot of Angers*. It is found in a ninth-century anthology at Verona, among verse for the most part godly. The metre is a trochaic line of eleven syllables, to be used again in the oldest Provençal *alba*, tenth century, and by William of Poitou in the eleventh: it had been used, as W. P. Ker points out, in the *Lorica* of Gildas of the sixth century, and is one of the famous Irish metres. Yet to claim it as the work of an Irish wandering scholar, some less respectable country-man of Sedulius, would be rash. The sons of Golias, the genial Pantagruelian prelate who bestrides the Middle Ages, had but one fatherland, *terra ridentium*, the country of the laughing.

Text in *Poet. Lat. Car.* iv. 591. For the *Cena*, see *ib.* 857 ff.: Novati, *Studi critici*, pp. 178 ff.

RADBOD   P. 130

d. 917

RADBOD, the son of a noble Frankish house, was brought up by his uncle Gunther, Archbishop of Cologne, to whom an Irish wandering scholar once addressed a flattering poem and wrote the rough draft on a blank page of his MS. of Priscian, where it abides to this day in St. Gall. Gunther was generous to vagabonds, but too sympathetic with human infirmity: he was deposed with the papal anathema, and his young nephew betook himself to the court of Charles the Bald, who had revived the tradition of Charlemagne's palace school, and thence to study under the Abbot Hugh of St. Martin's at Tours. In 899 he was elected Bishop of Utrecht, and consecrated in the following year. It was a troubled episcopate, for the irruption and devastation of the Danes drove him finally to Daventer; yet his memory remained at Utrecht in affection and reverence. He had that real austerity that dissembles itself in pleasantry: abstemious at table, but so gay in his speech that no man observed it. A friend of his, a layman, began however to suspect the contents of the great onyx goblet, adorned with gold, from which the Bishop drank, and asked leave to taste them, to the great confusion of the good man, who drank only water, but would not have it known, thinking it next to vice to parade a virtue. So he put off his friend with some excuse, but the importunate, still more inquisitive, watched his opportunity and took a mouthful by stealth: and thereby gave occasion to the kindliness of God, Who, perceiving the embarrassment of His servant, changed the water to a wine of singular bouquet. In a grave illness, the bishop was visited by the Blessed Virgin herself, with her two companions, Agnes and Thekla. Death came for him in the marshy country near Drenthe, a fever that burnt him out: he died, joyous and innocent as he had lived, with the *Laete* of his own antiphon in praise of the Blessed Martin upon his lips.

Texts edited by Paul von Winterfeld, *Poet. Lat. Car.* iv. pp. 161-2, 172-3. For the life, see *Mon. Germ. Hist. Scriptores*, xv. 568 ff. The Zwendebold of whom he speaks in his epitaph was king of Lorraine, and illegitimate son of Arnulf, one of the last of Charlemagne's house.

EUGENIUS VULGARIUS   P. 136

Fl. c. 907

VERY little is known of Eugenius Vulgarius except what can be deduced from his writings, that he was a timid and eager scholar devoted to Seneca, dreaming of a revival of learning that he did not live to see, an age of gold when Charlemagne would again be glorious, and Cato tell his tales and Apollo sing, and Seneca rehearse all splendid deeds, and Cicero speak with that organ voice again: that he took the losing side in a papal quarrel, wrote a vigorous and academic pamphlet, and fled ignominiously for shelter when the great cat spied him in his corner and reached out its claws.

Pope Formosus, in defence of whose dead majesty Vulgarius ventured for a short moment out of his obscurity, was the last great figure to occupy the Roman See before the squalid and ephemeral succession of the tenth-century popes. He had favoured Arnulf, one of the last princes of Charlemagne's house, in his claim to the Holy Roman Empire, as against the ducal house of Spoleto, too near and too violent a neighbour to the papal states; welcomed him when he invaded Italy in 896, and crowned him Emperor in Rome, in despite of the young duke Lambert and his deadly mother, Ageltrude. But Arnulf's luck was not with him. He was stricken by paralysis on the road to Spoleto, and drearily returned. A few days later, Formosus, now an old man of eighty, himself was dead.

Boniface VI, who succeeded him, was disposed of by poison in a fortnight: but Stephen VII, a personal enemy of Formosus, lent himself willingly to Ageltrude's vengeance. The dead Pope was exhumed, clad in his papal vestments and enthroned over against his enemy: formal trial was made, his consecration annulled, his body dishonoured, buried in the strangers' graveyard, and thence flung into the Tiber. All ordinations made by him were declared invalid, with what resultant satisfaction of petty greeds and local jealousies may be imagined. There was a swift reaction: Stephen was taken prisoner and strangled, and in 898, John IX, another of the short-lived popes, had the poor body, which the piety of some fishermen had rescued from the river, reinterred with all honour, and the findings of the ghastly trial reversed. But in 904, Sergius IV, an inveterate enemy of the Formosan party, again declared the consecration invalid. The whole question of the validity of orders arose, and in 907 poor Vulgarius took a hand in the quarrel, possibly because

Stephen, Bishop of Naples (who may have been his own bishop) was involved. *Non est sequax Petri, si non habeat meritum illius Petri* (He is not Peter's successor who hath not Peter's deserving) said Vulgarius boldly, thereby enunciating a principle that might well have shaken Christendom. It shook Sergius, who may have felt that he had little of Peter's merit. Vulgarius seems to have been ordered to a cell at Monte Cassino, and then, after a brief interval of quiet, summoned to Rome, which reduced him to the last extremity of terror. " The fear of death," said he, quoting Seneca, " is worse than death itself," and he wrote a quavering letter to Sergius' paternity. What should such a thing as he do, creeping beneath the feet of such great ones? " Behold, my corner pleaseth me well." Sergius seems to have felt that there was no further risk from that quarter, and let him be: there are shrill odes in praise of his magnificence. It is not an heroic story, but it is dangerous for mice to investigate the workings of the grindstones, and once at least his very defects, the scholar's timidity and wistfulness and anger at all the waste and cruelty of things, goaded him to a fragment of great and passionate verse.

Text in *Poet. Lat. Car.* iv. p. 433. See also Dümmler, *Auxilius und Vulgaris* (1866). Luitprand, *Antapodosis*, i. 28–31. Cf. the Pope's soliloquy in Browning's *The Ring and the Book.*

ALBA   P. 138

Tenth Century

THE manuscript Vatican Reg. 1462, a kind of dictionary of legal abbreviations, was written in the tenth century, and came with the Queen Christine MSS. to Rome. But its fame depends on three verses, exquisitely written in a tiny hand, though also of the tenth century, at the top right-hand corner of the generous margin. It is the first *alba*, the dawn-song to waken sleeping lovers,

"Oi, deus! oi deus! de l' alba, tant tost ve!"

and the refrain is one of the oldest fragments of Provençal, or of North Italy, for it is claimed for both. The handwriting is no clue, and the fact that the MS. is a legal one points as much to the secular schools of Northern Italy as to Fleury, to which the MS. was for some time ascribed. Some claim the *tenebras* for Mt. Tinibras of the Alpes Maritimes, and others that the difficult *bigil* is Vigil above Merano.

The text is from the facsimile in E. Monaci, *Facsimili di Antichi MSS.* (1892), p. 57. See also Monaci, *Rendiconti della Reale Accademia dei Lincei* (1892), pp. 475–487: W. P. Ker, *The Dark Ages*, 214.

ST. MICHAEL   P. 140

Tenth Century

THIS fragment of a sequence in honour of St. Michael is from the same tenth-century troper of St. Martial of Limoges (B.N. Lat. 1118) that holds *Iam dulcis amica.* Text in Dreves, *Analecta Hymnica Medii Aevi*, vii. p. 195, stanzas 6, 7.

VESTIUNT SILVE   P. 142

Tenth Century

THIS poem appears in very corrupt text in two manuscripts, a tenth-century MS. of Verona (Bibl. Cap. 88, f. 59²), and an eleventh-century MS. now in Cambridge, that formerly belonged to the monastery of St. Augustine at Canterbury. The latter has been edited with a facsimile text by Professor Breul in *The Cambridge Songs* (1913), and again with full critical notes and variants by Strecker, *Die Cambridger Lieder* (1926). It is one of the most important anthologies of gayer mediæval verse, and Professor Breul's conjecture that it was the song-book of some wandering scholar of the Rhine valley, copied by an English traveller in the Rhineland, or at Canterbury itself, is very agreeable. The handwriting is continental minuscule, with some Anglo-Saxon letters. The contents are an odd medley, fragments from Statius and Horace and Virgil, laments for dead emperors and bishops (of Treves, Cologne, Mainz), sequences for Easter and for St. Catharine, the patron saint of scholars, the song to the Nightingale and the admirable comedy of the Abbot John from Fulbert of Chartres, the famous " *O admirabile Veneris idolum* " from Verona, the impish fabliau of the *Snowchild*, the pious if also impish tale of the Abbess and the donkey, and half a dozen love songs, blackened with gall and scratched thin with the knife of some austere brother of St. Augustine's. But the *Vestiunt silvae* escaped him as harmless, redeemed as it was from vanity by the pious allegory of the last stanza. Already in the tenth century there is the kind of relaxing that one notes in the branches of the trees in February, inclining a little to the earth. Wipo the Presbyter who was born towards the end of it was a good ecclesiastic, but his proverb on the Love of the World to Come,

Si carcer talis, Deus, O tua mansio qualis ?
" If such Thy prison, Lord, what is Thy house of heaven ? "

is in the tradition of the humanists rather than the saints.

The text here given is a very unsatisfactory mosaic,

pieced from the facsimile MS., and the texts of Strecker and Breul.

l. 1. *merorem* is Haupt's emendation for the Cambridge *merorum*: Verona has, very reasonably, *ramorum*.

l. 7. *arridens* is Jaffe's suggestions for the Cambridge *arripens*: Verona has *arripiens*.

l. 13. *in auris* is Haupt's emendation for the Cambridge *in aeris*: Verona has *per agros*, but the sense is evidently the contrast between the lark's song in the high air and the very evident change in note as the downward flight begins.

l. 18. *fringultit*, Haupt's emendation for the Cambridge *gracellaris ultat*, from analogy with the poem on the voices of birds in *Anthologia Latina*, 762, l. 28.

l. 23. Dr. Montagu James suggests that the uncomfortably long line is due to a scribe incorporating the explanatory gloss *Maria* written above the *quae* of his original. His emendation is

nisi quae Christum baiulavit alvo.

IAM DULCIS AMICA   P. 144

Tenth Century

THIS first anticipation of Marlowe's *Come live with me and be my love* is the most famous and perhaps the oldest of the earlier mediæval love songs. It survives in three different musical settings: a tenth-century Vienna MS. (Cod. Vind. 116), formerly from Salzburg; the Cambridge MS. from St. Augustine of Canterbury; and a tenth-century MS. of St. Martial of Limoges, written during the reign of Hugh Capet (987–996), as is evident from the prayer for " Hugone a Deo coronato," and now in Paris (B.N. Lat. 1118). This last is a troper, remarkable for the beauty of its notation and its rough drawings of various musical instruments. The last two verses, where the smouldering coal breaks into flame, were omitted from the Limoges manuscript, and so it came that the good Dreves included it in his *Analecta Hymnica*, believing it, as Mr. Gaselee notes with very kindly malice, " in the innocence of his heart, to be a hymn to the Blessed Virgin, drawing much of its imagery from the *Song of Songs*." One of these dangerous verses was mutilated by the same hand that defaced the love-songs in the Cambridge MS. It is perhaps the happiest air from what Mr. Gaselee calls " the double flute of Ovid and the *Song of Songs* ": but compared with the sudden liquid break of

Ego fui sola in silva,

the rest of the poem has the shabbiness of last year's nests.

Text in Breul, *op. cit.* pp. 16, 64. See also Strecker, *op. cit.* p. 69, and Coussemaker, *Histoire de l'harmonie au moyen âge,* pl. viii. ix.

HERIGER, BISHOP OF MAINZ   P. 148

MS. *of the eleventh century*

HERIGER was Archbishop of Mainz from 913 to 927: and whether or not this story is apocryphal, it suggests the fine sardonic humour that befits a great ecclesiastic. Rabelais might have written it, and would have chosen a form not so very different. Du Méril suggests that the metre recalls the brief lines of old German poetry, linked by alliteration: and that the Latin version is possibly later than a popular song on the same subject. The " very thick woods " of this traveller's tale are as old as the search for Balder in the Scandinavian hell: and in Dante's *Inferno* there is *la dolorosa selva* of gnarled and poisoned trees. There is evidently a stanza lacking in which the prophet described St. Peter as *magister coquorum*, which was a charge of no small honour at a Frankish court.

The text is from Strecker, *Die Cambridger Lieder*, p. 65. See Du Méril, *Poésies populaires antérieures au XIIe siècle*, 298 ff.

LEVIS EXSURGIT ZEPHYRUS   P. 156

MS. of the eleventh century

THE only text of this lyric is in the MS. of St. Augustine: its sorrowfulness may have saved it from the gall that defaced the other love-songs. It is like nothing else in mediæval Latin. Most of the goliard songs are masculine, either mocking or pleading, and the famous fourteenth-century *Nun's complaint* is the vigorous protest of one who was of no nun's flesh and knew it. This has the wistfulness of early German Minnesong. In the *Capitulary of Charlemagne* of 789, it was prescribed that no abbess should allow her nuns to write or send *wini leodas*, love-songs.

The text is in Strecker, *op. cit.* p. 95. On *wini leodas* see Lot, *Archiv. Med. Lat.*, 1925, 102 ff.

SIGEBERT OF GEMBLOUX   P. 158

c. 1030–1112

THERE were two places in Europe in the eleventh century where the Latin lyric metres were written with ease and pleasure: in Salerno and Liége. Sigebert came in his youth to the monastery at Gembloux, near Liége, where Olbert whom he greatly loved was abbot: he left it at his master's death to go to St. Vincent's, and be master of the schools at Metz. All men liked him, says the admiring disciple who wrote his life, " even the Jews," because he was interested in Hebrew, and had long talks with them about St. Jerome's translation from the Hebrew, not the LXX. But, finally, *ut apis prudentissima, ad monasterii sui alvearia*, returning as a wise bee to his own monastic hive, he came back to the house of his youth, and there abode till his death. There he taught " me and many my betters," says the same disciple: and always there was an air about him " of antique knowledge and reverence." A moderate man in all things, even in practice of austerity: " a discreet mediocrity," was his aim, says the biographer, not realizing how good a phrase he had come upon, nor that it perhaps explained why his master was so great a lover of Horace. He lived to be very old and frail, but his mind lost nothing of its edge: and when the time of his death drew near, the brethren took counsel as to whether they might not bury him in the monastery itself, presumably in the church, that they might keep their scholar: but he, disliking ostentation or anything that might seem particular, begged to lie with his brethren in the graveyard: and it was done. His fame is rather for his Chronicles than his poetry: he was an exact historian, careful in his use of sources, and meticulous in stating them. But it is in the poems that his personality escapes, a lover of fields and of open air and of walking, and alive to the greatness of lives more heroic and passionate than his. His *St. Lucy* was inspired by the presence of the holy relics at Metz, the last stage of their long journey from Sicily, but the *Martyrdom of the Theban Legion*, the patron saints of his monastery, has the same generous passion for the unnamed dead that moved Prudentius, kneeling before the " unnumbered ashes " of the martyrs in Rome.

The text of *Hinc virginalis sancta frequentia* is in Dümmler's edition of the *Passio Sanctae Luciae*, stanzas 16, 17, 19

(*Abhandl. d. Kgl. Akad.*, Berlin, Philo.-hist. Klasse, 1893), written in alcaics, as Sigebert himself noted; *Conatus roseas*, the epilogue of the *Passio Sanctorum Thebeorum*, ll. 1054–1077, in heroics, also edited by Dümmler. For his life see *M.G.H. SS.* vi. pp. 268 ff.

PETER ABELARD   P. 162

1079–1142

NOTHING is left of all the verse that Abelard wrote for Heloise and set to airs so lovely that even the unlettered knew his name. Long after, when the tempest was quiet and she was abbess of the Paraclete, she wrote to him, begging that he would write hymns for her sisterhood to sing. He was for a long time opposed to it, saying that it seemed to him almost sacrilege to prefer new-fangled hymns of sinful men to the venerable rhythms of the saints, but with many reasons, such as uncertainty of ascription, and the unaptness of some of the older measures to the tune, and the lack on certain high-days of any hymn at all, she prevailed on him, and he wrote the collection of ninety-three hymns, which forms part of the Breviary of the Paraclete. *Solus ad victimam* (Alone to sacrifice Thou goest, Lord) is the supreme expression of his faith, and of that theory of the Atonement which his century branded as heresy, and which is the beginning of modern theology.

The lament of David for Jonathan belongs to another collection, found by Greith in the Vatican and published by him in his *Spicilegium Vaticanum* in 1830. There are six in all, the lament of Dinah for her ruined lover, questioning if the urgency of love might not be a kind of sanctification for the fault; the lament of Jacob for his sons; of the daughters of Israel for Jephthah's daughter dead in her

327

virginity, with its strange likeness to the Heloise whom he had forced to take the veil: the lament of Israel over Samson, with its sudden arrest at the abyss of the judgments of God; of David over Abner, destroyed by guile; and greatest of all, the lament for Jonathan, where the passion that never escaped in those strange remote letters to Heloise for once awakes and cries.

Texts in Dreves, *P. Abelardi hymnarius Paraclitensis* (Paris, 1891), pp. 62, 65. The *Planctus* is in Meyer, *Romanische Forschungen*, 1890, p. 433, ll. 73–92, 105–110. See also Carnandet, *Notice sur le bréviaire d'Abailard* (1852).

THE ARCHPOET P. 170

Died c. 1165

ALL that is known of the Archpoet is a matter of inference and deduction from his meagre bundle of ten poems. He travelled light, even to immortality. Fortunately his patron, Reginald von Dassel, Archbishop of Cologne and Chancellor to Frederick Barbarossa, was a figure massive and splendid enough to kindle Otto von Freisingen's imagination, and from the time that Reginald came on his first embassy to the Pope till his death of the plague before Rome in the fatal campaign of 1167, the record is clear and full. Not full enough, however, to include the comings and goings of a rather disreputable figure, keen as a razor and lean as a hawk, with the Chancellor's own cloak hugged about his tatters and his narrow consumptive shoulders.

That figure first sidled up to the Chancellor during his mission to Rome, making unflattering comments on the parsimony of Italian ecclesiastics, and indicating that it also was an exile in Italy, and had a bad cough and a rapid pulse. One next finds it swaggering in the Chancellor's cloak in the refectory of some Alpine monastery, but not above taking up a collection from the brethren. Thereafter he seems more or less permanently attached, if either word can be used of so volatile a spirit, to the Chancellor's train, in very high feather, with a fine horse, and money to spend, and the Emperor himself applauding one of his songs. There is a dreadful moment of disgrace, thanks to some scandal about a wench, and for a while the Archpoet is again on the road, *trutannizans* and hankering sadly. A sheer *tour de force* of penitent rhyming melts the Chancellor's displeasure into laughter; but there is some talk of making the Archpoet respectable, and giving him a profession, medicine for instance, at Salerno. So the Archpoet trundles obediently down south, but in a few months is back again, leaner and more disreputable than ever, burnt out with fever, and quite resolute against further pursuit of his studies. The year 1165 finds him undismayed in the infirmary of St. Martin's cloister at Cologne, detailing his symptoms with the old relish, and balancing with the old airiness, but this time on eternity. It had no terrors for him: had not Augustine chatted with him about the nature of universals on the occasion of his last visit to heaven, and Michael meeting him on his way out talked to him as man to man? True, he was sorry to miss Homer and Aristotle there. Meantime, the Abbot is his good shepherd, and whoever comes short, for him there is no stint in the wine. With that the darkness swallows him, and the Archpoet becomes what he has been ever since in literature, a reckless and gallant ghost.

It is on the *Confessio*, however, that his reputation rests. It is one of the hardiest things in mediæval literature, the first articulate reasoned rebellion against the denying of the body, though a few years earlier Bernard Sylvestris had been teaching something of its dignity at Tours. The

Confessio was written at Pavia, whose university celebrated its eleventh centenary in May 1925, in commemoration of its founding by Lothair, under Dungal the Irishman, as centre of the minor schools of Lombardy. It was already three hundred years in existence when Reginald made it occasional headquarters during the years of the breaking of Milan, and the *Gaudeamus igitur* that rings at dusk through most old university towns was here more insistent than the *Angelus.* Reginald, for all his youth and magnificence, was a stern ascetic: " he showed no mercy to himself," says Otto, " for lust or for default." At Vienne, the Archpoet had had to fly his presence: here, he challenged his accusers and turned at bay.

The result of it was the poem that created a literary kind in Europe, and is the greatest drinking song in the world. It is the first defiance by the artist of that society which it is his thankless business to amuse: the first cry from the House of the Potter, " Why hast thou made me thus? "

For the text, see Manitius, *Die Gedichte des Archipoeta* (1913). See also Schmeidler, *Die Gedichte des Archipoeta* (1911): Grimm, *Gedichte des Mittelalters auf König Friedrich den Staufer* (*Kleinere Schriften*, iii. 1844).

MS. OF BENEDICTBEUERN   P. 184

Carmina Burana

THIS manuscript, the most famous anthology of mediæval lyric yet discovered, was found in the Hof-Bibliothek at Munich in the beginning of the last century: it had come there with other flotsam after the dissolution of the monastery of Benedictbeuern in Upper Bavaria. Even there, it had never appeared in the library catalogue, but seems to have lived a kind of stowaway existence, hidden to save it from the censor's gall. The handwriting is of the thirteenth century; forty-three of the poems are noted to be sung. It was not a commonplace book, growing by haphazard jottings, but a copy made by three distinct hands and at one time, from various originals, one of them evidently a scholar's song-book. In the judgment of its latest editors, the manuscript was written in Bavaria, possibly in Benedictbeuern, towards the close of the century. The contents were roughly grouped, the smaller and graver section including complaints on fortune, attacks on simony, for the unbeneficed have always been harsh with the beneficed, recruiting songs for the Crusades,

" Man, have pity upon God,"

a pæan on the ending of the schism in 1177, a lament for the terrible defeat in Palestine in 1187, and for the death of Richard Cœur-de-Lion in 1199: at the end of the MS., two plays, for Christmas and for Easter, a good deal more elaborate than those which the vagabond Hilarius took about with him in the earlier half of the twelfth century. The other and by far the more famous group is a collection of love-songs, drinking songs, songs in praise of the vaga-bond order, a very profane Gamblers' Mass, and a few begging songs, one very neat, with a blank left as in the catechism for the name of the person addressed, *Decus N.*, as who should say, " O Pride of Coventry,"—or Canter-bury, or Cologne, or Salzburg. As for provenance, the " shaping spirit " is German, and the German lyrics scattered through it have the freshness of young beech leaves: the Latin lyrics belong to the scholars' common-wealth, of Paris and Orleans and Oxford, Bologna and Salerno and Pavia. Fragments from the *Copa* and from Ovid jostle with songs from Hugh of Orleans, from the Archpoet, from Walther von der Vogelweide, from Gautier de Châtillon, possibly from Abelard himself: but most of them are anonymous, *herrenlos* as the German has it, like their authors masterless men. For the wandering clerks, like the Latin tongue, knew no frontiers: " Swift and unstable as the swallows . . . hither, thither, like a leaf caught up by the wind or a spark in the brushwood, we wander, unweariedly weary."

Yet diverse as the authors are, the book has a unity, as though scattered drops of quicksilver had come together, and the figure that emerges from it is oddly familiar. The background of their century, Barbarossa and Thomas Becket, the second Henry and the second Frederick, Paris University and Chartres Cathedral dissolve and pass " indistinct, As water is in water," just as in the half-melancholy wizardry of the last scene in *Twelfth Night* the Duke and the lovers, the priest and the Puritan go by, and leave only ' Mimus whistling to his tabouret,'

> "A great while ago the world began,
>   With hey, ho, the wind and the rain."

But here there is no melancholy, and very little of the wind and rain—

> *In taberna quando sumus*
> *Non curamus quid sit humus.*

It seems not possible that poetry should be so gay as this. These poets are young, as Keats and Shelley and Swinburne never were young, with the youth of wavering branches and running water. They do not look before and after, they make light of frozen thawings and of ruined springs, and if they came in the end to write their Ecclesiastes, the man who compiled this anthology has kept record only of their youth.

The MS. was clumsily edited by Schmeller in his *Carmina Burana* (Stuttgart, 1847), but a critical text by Alfons Hilka and Otto Schumann is in preparation, of which the first two sections are already available (*Carmina Burana*, hrsg. A. Hilka and O. Schumann, Bde. 1, 2. Winter, Heidelberg, 1930). See also F. Lüers, *Die deutschen Lieder der Carmina Burana* (Bonn, 1922); Wilhelm Meyer, *Fragmenta Burana* (*Festschrift der Kgl. Gesellsch. . . . zu Göttingen, Abhandl. philo-hist. Klasse*, 1901); Ulich and Manitius, *Vagantenlieder aus der lateinischen Dichtung des* 12. *und* 13. *Jahrhunderts* (Jena, 1927).

P. 184. *Potatores exquisiti* (To you, consummate drinkers). Text in *Carmina Burana*, 179, p. 240. The mixing of wine with water was anathema in vagabond verse: and a tractate which Primas of Cologne made against it was a great favourite with Philip, Archbishop of Ravenna.

P. 188. *Fas et Nefas ambulant* (Right and Wrong, they go about). *Carmina Burana*, ii, p. 2; Hilka-Schumann, 19.

P. 192. *Dic Christi Veritas* (O Truth of Christ). *Carmina Burana*, xciii, p. 51. About a third of the Benedictbeuern MS. is serious, some of it devout, but for the most part satirical. The satire of the *Vagantes*, most of them scholars disappointed of preferment, or "spoiled priests," was one of the earliest corrosives of the mediæval church. This, however, is ascribed to Philippe de Grève.

P. 196. *Veritas veritatum*. *Carm. Bur.* iii, p. 3; Hilka-Schumann, 21.

P. 198. *Omne genus demoniorum* (Every one of demon race). *Carm. Bur.* xxx, p. 35; Hilka-Schumann, 55.

P. 202. *Obmittamus studia* (Let's away with study). *Carm. Bur.* 48, p. 137.

P. 206. *Terra iam pandit gremium* (The earth lies openbreasted). *Carm. Bur.* 103, p. 181.

P. 210. *Cedit, hyems, tua durities* (Now, winter, yieldeth all thy dreariness). *Carm. Bur.* 98, p. 177.

P. 212. *Iamiam rident prata* (Now the fields are laughing). *Carm. Bur.* 107, p. 184.

P. 214. *Letabundus rediit* (Joyously return again). *Carm. Bur.* 47, p. 136. Text in Manitius, *Vagantenlieder*, p. 2.

P. 218. *Ab estatis foribus* (At the gates of summer). *Carm. Bur.* cii, p. 91.

P. 220. *Estas non apparuit* (Never ancient summer). *Carm. Bur.* 115, p. 190.

P. 222. *Tempus est iocundum* (Now's the time for pleasure). *Carm. Bur.* 140, p. 211. Text in Manitius, *op. cit.*, p. 6.

P. 228. *Volo virum vivere viriliter* (I would have a man live in manly fashion). *Carm. Bur.* 139, p. 210.

P. 232. *Salve ver optatum* (O Spring, the long desired). *Carm. Bur.* 118, p. 193.

P. 234. *Ecce, chorus virginum* (Here be maids dancing). *Carm. Bur.* 34, p. 118.

P. 238. *Musa venit carmine* (Gay comes the singer). *Carm. Bur.* 108, p. 185.

P. 242. *Clausus Chronos* (Time's shut up). *Carm. Bur.* 46, p. 135. The popular confusion of Chronos and Cronos, Time and Saturn, is noted by Paulinus of Nola, *Carm.* xxxii, 191. The *Esto Dione* of the last line is Sir Frederick Pollock's emendation of *Es et Dione*, which was in turn an emendation of Schmeller's

> *Et quibus est Venus,*
> *Est et Dione.*

P. 246. *Nobilis, mei miserere precor* (Noblest, I pray thee). *Carm. Bur.* 166, p. 228.

P. 250. *Prata iam rident omnia* (O sweet are flowers to gather). *Carm. Bur.* 165, p. 228.

P. 252. *Suscipe Flos florem* (Take thou this rose, O Rose). *Carm. Bur.* 147, p. 217.

P. 254. *O comes amoris dolor* (O Sorrow, that art still Love's company). *Carm. Bur.* 162, p. 225. Also in Wilhelm Meyer, *Fragmenta Burana*, from another manuscript, with additional stanzas, and variants not always for the better; the conventional *urit amor*, for instance, instead of *dolor urget*, *exitium* for *exilium*.

P. 256. *Anni novi rediit novitas* (New Year has brought renewing). *Carm. Bur.* 51, p. 145. Is the *Francie regina* Eleanor of Aquitaine, before the divorce from Louis VII made her Queen of England?

P. 258. *Dira vi amoris teror* (By the dread force of love). *Carm. Bur.* 158, p. 223.

P. 262. *Dum estas inchoatur* (While summer on is stealing). *Carm. Bur.* 122, p. 196.

P. 264. *Dum Diane vitrea* (When Diana lighteth). *Carm. Bur.* 37, p. 124. Text in Manitius, *Vagantenlieder*, p. 22.

P. 268. *Sic mea fata canendo solor* (So by my singing am I comforted). *Carm. Bur.* 167, p. 229.

P. 272. *Estas in exilium* (Summer to a strange land). *Carm. Bur.* 42, p. 131.

DE RAMIS CADUNT FOLIA   P. 274

c. 1200

THIS is one of the rare though almost invariably beautiful love-songs written in winter, not in spring. It is from a thirteenth-century manuscript (B.N. Lat. 3719) which also holds the almost Elizabethan melody of *Sic mea fata canendo solor* (" So by my singing am I comforted "). The translation of the last stanza is perhaps insufferably free: and yet it is not, I think, very far from the meaning of the original conceit: " Greek fire is extinguished by bitter wine (i.e. vinegar), but this of mine (*hic ignis* of stanza 4) is not extinguished by the poorest: nay rather, it is fed on fuel most rich." Or, in other and more famous words,

> " O Love! they wrong thee much
> That say thy sweet is bitter,
> When thy rich fruit is such
> As nothing can be sweeter."

It is possible that *miserrimo* refers not to wine, but to *mihi* understood: yet this is to deface the triumph of the poem.

Text in Du Méril, *Poésies populaires latines du moyen âge* (1847), p. 235.

IPSA VIVERE MIHI REDDIDIT   P. 278

c. 1200

THE Arundel MS. 384 from which this poem is taken is one of the four great collections of mediæval lyric. It is written in English cursive script of the second half of the fourteenth century, and falls into three sections, love-lyric, praise of Christ and his Mother, and satires against the higher clergy. It belongs to the great age of Latin lyric, between 1150 and 1250, and the intricacy of rhyme and metre beguiles but defies the translator. Thomas Wright (of inaccurate and blessed memory) first published them, and hoped that he might claim them for England. One, the second to last, is in praise of a great English " pontifex," gay in speech, and learned in living, and subtly wise in rendering unto Cæsar the things that are Cæsar's, to God the things that are God's. Meyer suggests an ecclesiastic who was also a Chancellor: and one is tempted to give the poem to some anonymous lover of Thomas Becket, in the days before Cæsar and he were at odds. Five poems from this anthology appear also in the *Carmina Burana*.

Text in W. Meyer, *Die Arundel Sammlung Mittellateinischer Lieder* (Abhandlung. d. Kgl. Akad. zu Göttingen: philosoph.-hist. Klasse 1909), p. 25.

INDEX OF AUTHORS AND MSS.

INDEX TO FIRST LINES (ENGLISH)

339

INDEX TO FIRST LINES (LATIN)